Sphinx Search
Beginner's Guide

Implement full-text search with lightning speed and accuracy
using Sphinx

Abbas Ali

BIRMINGHAM - MUMBAI

Sphinx Search
Beginner's Guide

First published: March 2011

Production Reference: 1100311

Published by Packt Publishing Ltd.
32 Lincoln Road
Olton
Birmingham, B27 6PA, UK.

ISBN 978-1-849512-54-1

www.packtpub.com

Cover Image by Asher Wishkerman (a.wishkerman@mpic.de)

Credits

Author
Abbas Ali

Reviewers
Paul Grinberg

Kevin Horn

Acquisition Editor
Eleanor Duffy

Development Editor
Roger D'souza

Technical Editor
Aaron Rosario

Indexers
Tejal Daruwale

Monica Ajmera Mehta

Editorial Team Leader
Aanchal Kumar

Project Team Leader
Priya Mukherji

Project Coordinator
Sneha Harkut

Proofreader
Jonathan Russell

Graphics
Nilesh Mohite

Production Coordinator
Melwyn D'sa

Cover Work
Melwyn D'sa

About the Author

Abbas Ali has over six years of experience in PHP Development and is a Zend Certified PHP 5 Engineer. A Mechanical Engineer by education, Abbas turned to software development just after finishing his engineering degree. He is a member of the core development team for the Coppermine Photo Gallery, an open source project, which is one of the most popular photo gallery applications in the world.

Fascinated with both machines and knowledge, Abbas is always learning new programming techniques. He got acquainted with Sphinx in 2009 and has been using it in most of his commercial projects ever since. He loves open source and believes in contributing back to the community.

Abbas is married to Tasneem and has a cute little daughter, Munira. He has lived in Nagpur (India) since his birth and is in no rush to move to any other city in the world. In his free time he loves to watch movies and television. He is also an amateur photographer and cricketer.

Abbas is currently working as Chief Operating Officer and Technical Manager at SANIsoft Technologies Private Limited, Nagpur, India. The company specializes in development of large, high performance, and scalable PHP applications.

For feedback and suggestions, you can contact Abbas at:

Web : http://www.abbasali.net/contact/

Twitter: @_abbas

Acknowledgement

My wife Tasneem and sweet little daughter Munira were patient throughout my writing adventure, and I want to thank them for giving me tremendous support and quiet space to work at home. I would also like to thank my mother for her moral support.

My inspiration was Dr. Tarique Sani, CTO of SANIsoft, who is my employer, mentor, and guru. I would like to thank him for his support and exchange of technical know-how. I would also like to thank my colleagues at SANIsoft who encouraged me in my endeavor.

I would also like to thank all the reviewers and editors who worked patiently with me. A special thanks to Aaron Rosario who worked sleepless nights during the final editing phase.

Richard Phillips of Utilitas Knowledge Management Limited, London, introduced me to Sphinx while I was working on one of his projects in 2009. He deserves special thanks and acknowledgment.

Last, but not the least; I would like to thank my brother who has been an inspiration all my life.

About the Reviewers

Paul Grinberg is an electrical engineer with a focus on embedded firmware design. As part of his work he has utilized many techniques that traditionally fall outside of his field, including a number of scripting languages. While learning PHP, Paul started contributing to the MediaWiki project by writing a number of extensions. One of those extensions was the Sphinx Search extension to improve the search capability of the MediaWiki engine.

> I would like to thank Svemir Brkic, who is the co-author of the Sphinx Search extension for MediaWiki. I would also like to thank my wife for her understanding, flexibility, and support for my hobbies.

Kevin Horn has a B.S. in Mechanical Engineering from Texas A&M University and has been creating web applications since 1998, when he accidentally became a web developer after running out of money for college. He's worked under almost every job title in the IT field, though he always seems to come back to programming. Despite working with a number of different languages, there's no doubt that his favorite is Python, as he will tell anyone who will listen (and some who won't).

Kevin lives in North Texas with his wife, two sons, and a couple of canine interlopers.

Kevin currently works as a semi-freelance programmer both through his own company and others. In his not-so-copious free time, he works on various open source Python projects, reads a truly ridiculous amount of fiction, and tries to figure out how to raise his offspring properly.

> Thanks to the Packt team for making the process of reviewing my first book pretty darn painless. I'd also like to thank my wife, kids, and friends for putting up with me staring at the computer screen, when they'd much rather I be doing something else.

www.PacktPub.com

Support files, eBooks, discount offers, and more

You might want to visit www.PacktPub.com for support files and downloads related to your book.

Did you know that Packt offers eBook versions of every book published, with PDF and ePub files available? You can upgrade to the eBook version at www.PacktPub.com and as a print book customer, you are entitled to a discount on the eBook copy. Get in touch with us at service@packtpub.com for more details.

At www.PacktPub.com, you can also read a collection of free technical articles, sign up for a range of free newsletters and receive exclusive discounts and offers on Packt books and eBooks.

http://PacktLib.PacktPub.com

Do you need instant solutions to your IT questions? PacktLib is Packt's online digital book library. Here, you can access, read, and search across Packt's entire library of books.

Why Subscribe?

- Fully searchable across every book published by Packt
- Copy and paste, print and bookmark content
- On demand and accessible via web browser

Free Access for Packt account holders

If you have an account with Packt at www.PacktPub.com, you can use this to access PacktLib today and view nine entirely free books. Simply use your login credentials for immediate access.

Table of Contents

Preface	1

Chapter 1: Setting Up Sphinx — 7

What you need to know	8
Different ways of performing a search	8
Searching on a live database	8
Searching an index	9
Sphinx—a full-text search engine	10
Features	10
A brief history	10
License	11
Installation	11
System requirements	11
Sphinx on a Unix-based system	12
Time for action – installation on Linux	12
Options to the configure command	13
Known issues during installation	14
Sphinx on Windows	14
Time for action – installation on Windows	14
Sphinx on Mac OS X	15
Time for action – installation on a Mac	15
Other supported systems	16
Summary	17

Chapter 2: Getting Started — 19

Checking the installation	19
Full-text search	21
What is full-text search?	21
Traditional search	21

Time for action – normal search in MySQL	**21**
MySQL full-text search	24
Advantages of full-text search	25
When to use a full-text search?	25
Overview of Sphinx	**25**
Primary programs	25
Time for action – Sphinx in action	**26**
Data to be indexed	30
Creating the Sphinx configuration file	31
Searching the index	31
Why use Sphinx for full-text searching?	**32**
Summary	**33**
Chapter 3: Indexing	**35**
What are indexes?	**35**
Indexes in Sphinx	36
Index attributes	**37**
Types of attributes	37
Multi-value attributes (MVA)	38
Data sources	**38**
How to define the data source?	39
SQL data sources	39
Creating Index using SQL data source (Blog)	41
Time for action – creating database tables for a blog	**42**
Time for action – populate the database tables	**43**
Time for action – creating the Sphinx configuration file	**45**
Time for action – adding attributes to the index	**50**
Time for action – Adding an MVA to the index	**53**
xmlpipe data source	56
xmlpipe2 data source	56
Indexing with schema defined in XML stream	57
Time for action – creating index (without attributes)	**57**
Time for action – add attributes to schema	**62**
Indexing with schema defined in configuration file	67
Time for action – create index with schema defined in configuration file	**67**
Summary	**71**
Chapter 4: Searching	**73**
Client API implementations for Sphinx	**73**
Search using client API	**74**
Time for action – creating a basic search script	**74**
Matching modes	79

Time for action – searching with different matching modes   **80**
  Boolean query syntax   86
Time for action – searching using Boolean query syntax   **87**
  Extended query syntax   90
Time for action – searching with extended query syntax   **90**
Filtering full-text search results   **95**
Time for action – filtering the result set   **95**
Weighting search results   **99**
Time for action – weighting search results   **99**
Sorting modes   **102**
Grouping search results   **103**
Summary   **104**

Chapter 5: Feed Search   **105**
The application   **105**
  Tools and software used while creating this application   106
  Database structure   106
Time for action – creating the MySQL database and tables   **106**
  Basic setup   108
Time for action – setting up the feeds application   **108**
  Add feed   111
Time for action – creating a form to add feeds   **111**
  Saving the feed data   114
Time for action – adding code to save feed   **114**
  Indexing the feeds   117
Time for action – create the index   **117**
  Check for duplicate items   122
Time for action – adding code to avoid duplicate items   **122**
  Index merging   124
Time for action – adding the delta index   **124**
  Search form   126
Time for action – creating the search form   **126**
  Perform the search query   128
Time for action – adding code to perform a search query   **128**
  Applying filters   133
Time for action – adding code to filter the results   **133**
Time for action – showing search form prefilled with last submitted data   **134**
  Re-indexing   137
Summary   **137**

Chapter 6: Property Search	**139**
The application	**139**
Tools and software used while creating this application	140
Database structure	141
Time for action – creating the MySQL database and structure	**141**
Initial data	144
Time for action – populating the database	**144**
Basic setup	145
Time for action – setting up the application	**145**
Adding a property	149
Time for action – creating the form to add property	**149**
Indexing the properties	155
Time for action – creating the index	**155**
Simple search form	158
Time for action – creating the simple search form	**158**
Full-text search	160
Time for action – adding code to perform full-text search	**160**
Advanced search	163
Time for action – creating the Advanced search form	**163**
Ranged filters	167
Time for action – adding ranged filters	**167**
Geo distance search	172
Time for action – creating the search form	**172**
Add geo anchor	174
Time for action – adding code to perform geo distance search	**174**
Summary	**179**
Chapter 7: Sphinx Configuration	**181**
Sphinx configuration file	**181**
Rules for creating the configuration file	182
Data source configuration	**184**
SQL related options	184
Connection options	184
Options to fetch data (SQL data source)	186
Configuration file using advanced options	187
Time for action – creating a configuration with advanced source options	**187**
MS SQL specific options	189
Index configuration	**190**
Distributed searching	190
Set up an index on multiple servers	190

Time for action – creating indexes for distributed searching   **191**
    Set up the distributed index on the primary server   194
Time for action – adding distributed index configuration   **195**
    Distributed searching on single server   197
  charset configuration   198
  Data related options   199
  Word processing options   201
    Morphology   201
Time for action – using morphology for stemming   **202**
    Wordforms   204
Search daemon configuration   **204**
Indexer configuration   **207**
Summary   **208**
Chapter 8: What Next?   **209**
SphinxQL   **209**
  SphinxQL in action   209
Time for action – querying Sphinx using MySQL CLI   **210**
  SELECT   212
    Column list clause   212
    SHOW WARNINGS   215
    SHOW STATUS   216
    SHOW META   216
Use case scenarios   **217**
Popular websites using Sphinx   **218**
Summary   **218**
Index   **219**

Preface

This book will serve as a guide to everything that you need to know about running a Sphinx Search Engine. In today's world, search is an integral part of any application; a reliable search engine like Sphinx Search can be the difference between running a successful and unsuccessful business. What good is being on the web if no one knows you are there? It's easy to build a proficient search engine, with Sphinx Search: Beginners Guide at hand.

What this book covers

Chapter 1, Setting Up Sphinx is an introduction to Sphinx. It guides the reader through the installation process for Sphinx on all major operating systems.

Chapter 2, Getting Started demonstrates some basic usage of Sphinx in order to test its installation. It also discusses full-text search and gives the reader an overview of Sphinx.

Chapter 3, Indexing teaches the reader how to create indexes. It introduces and explains the different types of datasources, and also discusses different types of attributes that can comprise an index.

Chapter 4, Searching teaches the reader how to use the Sphinx Client API to search indexes from within PHP applications. It shows the reader how to use the PHP implementation of the Sphinx Client API.

Chapter 5, Feed Search creates an application that fetches feed items and creates a Sphinx index. This index is then searched from a PHP application. It also introduces delta indexes and live index merging.

Chapter 6, Property Search creates a real world real estate portal where the user can add a property listing and specify different attributes for it so that you can search for properties based on specific criteria. Some advanced search techniques using a client API are discussed in this chapter.

Chapter 7, Sphinx Configuration discusses all commonly used configuration settings for Sphinx. It teaches the reader how to configure Sphinx in a distributed environment where indexes are kept on multiple machines.

Chapter 8, What Next? discusses some new features introduced in the recent Sphinx release. It also shows the reader how a Sphinx index can be searched using a MySQL client library. Lastly, it discusses the scenarios where Sphinx can be used and mentions some of the popular Web applications that are powered by a Sphinx search engine.

Who this book is for

This book is for developers who are new to Sphinx Search. All code examples use PHP but the underlying logic is the same for any other web scripting language.

Conventions

In this book, you will find several headings appearing frequently.

To give clear instructions of how to complete a procedure or task, we use:

Time for action – heading

1. Action 1
2. Action 2
3. Action 3

Instructions often need some extra explanation so that they make sense, so they are followed with:

What just happened?

This heading explains the working of tasks or instructions that you have just completed.

You will also find some other learning aids in the book, including:

Pop quiz – heading

These are short multiple choice questions intended to help you test your own understanding.

Have a go hero – heading

These set practical challenges and give you ideas for experimenting with what you have learned.

You will also find a number of styles of text that distinguish between different kinds of information. Here are some examples of these styles, and an explanation of their meaning.

Code words in text are shown as follows: "We can include other contexts through the use of the `include` directive."

A block of code is set as follows:

```
# searchd options (used by search daemon)
searchd
{
  listen          = 9312
  log             = /usr/local/sphinx/var/log/searchd.log
  query_log       = /usr/local/sphinx/var/log/query.log
  max_children    = 30
  pid_file        = /usr/local/sphinx/var/log/searchd.pid
}
```

When we wish to draw your attention to a particular part of a code block, the relevant lines or items are set in bold:

```
source blog {
  # source options
}

index posts {
  # index options
}
```

Any command-line input or output is written as follows:

```
$ mkdir /path/to/your/webroot/sphinx
```

New terms and **important words** are shown in bold. Words that you see on the screen, in menus or dialog boxes for example, appear in the text like this: "clicking on the **Next** button moves you to the next screen".

Warnings or important notes appear in a box like this.

Tips and tricks appear like this.

Reader feedback

Feedback from our readers is always welcome. Let us know what you think about this book—what you liked or may have disliked. Reader feedback is important for us to develop titles that you really get the most out of.

To send us general feedback, simply send an e-mail to feedback@packtpub.com, and mention the book title via the subject of your message.

If there is a book that you need and would like to see us publish, please send us a note in the **SUGGEST A TITLE** form on www.packtpub.com or e-mail suggest@packtpub.com.

If there is a topic that you have expertise in and you are interested in either writing or contributing to a book, see our author guide on www.packtpub.com/authors.

Customer support

Now that you are the proud owner of a Packt book, we have a number of things to help you to get the most from your purchase.

Downloading the example code for this book

You can download the example code files for all Packt books you have purchased from your account at http://www.PacktPub.com. If you purchased this book elsewhere, you can visit http://www.PacktPub.com/support and register to have the files e-mailed directly to you.

Errata

Although we have taken every care to ensure the accuracy of our content, mistakes do happen. If you find a mistake in one of our books—maybe a mistake in the text or the code—we would be grateful if you would report this to us. By doing so, you can save other readers from frustration and help us improve subsequent versions of this book. If you find any errata, please report them by visiting http://www.packtpub.com/support, selecting your book, clicking on the **errata submission form** link, and entering the details of your errata. Once your errata are verified, your submission will be accepted and the errata will be uploaded on our website, or added to any list of existing errata, under the Errata section of that title. Any existing errata can be viewed by selecting your title from http://www.packtpub.com/support.

Piracy

Piracy of copyright material on the Internet is an ongoing problem across all media. At Packt, we take the protection of our copyright and licenses very seriously. If you come across any illegal copies of our works, in any form, on the Internet, please provide us with the location address or website name immediately so that we can pursue a remedy.

Please contact us at copyright@packtpub.com with a link to the suspected pirated material.

We appreciate your help in protecting our authors, and our ability to bring you valuable content.

Questions

You can contact us at questions@packtpub.com if you are having a problem with any aspect of the book, and we will do our best to address it.

1
Setting Up Sphinx

Search is by far the most important feature of an application where data is stored and retrieved. If it hadn't been for search, Google wouldn't exist, so we can imagine the importance of search in the computing world.

Search can be found in the following types of applications:

- **Desktop applications**: Where you are the primary, and most often, the only user
- **Web applications**: Where the application or website is used and visited by many users

For desktop applications, search is a quick way of locating files. Most desktop applications are not data-oriented, that is, they are not meant to organize and display information. They are rather meant to perform certain tasks, making search a secondary feature.

When using a web application, more often than not, the search becomes a means to navigate the website and look for things that we are interested in, things which are otherwise hidden deep inside the site's structure. Search becomes more important if the web application is full of rich-text content such as blogs, articles, knowledge bases, and so on; where a user needs the search functionality to find a particular piece of information.

In this chapter we will:

- Discuss different ways to search for data
- See how Sphinx helps us in achieving our goal
- Learn how to install Sphinx

So let's get on with it...

What you need to know

For this chapter, it is important that you know basic Linux commands (if you intend to install sphinx on a Linux machine). If you use Windows then you should have a basic idea of how to install programs in Windows.

Different ways of performing a search

Searching can be done in different ways but here we will take a look at the two most commonly used methods.

Searching on a live database

Whenever your application is dealing with some kind of data, a database is generally involved. There are many databases (both free and commercial) available in the market. Here are a few of the free and open source database servers available:

- MySQL
- PostgreSQL
- SQLite

 We will be using MySQL throughout this book since Sphinx supports MySQL by default, and it's also the most popular database when it comes to web development.

A **live database** is one that is actively updated with the latest version of data. At times you may use one database for reading and another for writing, and in such cases you will sync both the databases occasionally. We cannot call such a database 'live', because when reading from one database, while data is being written to the other database, you won't be reading the latest data.

On the other hand, whenever reading from and writing to the database takes place in real-time, we call it a live database.

Let's take an example to understand how search works in the case of a live database.

Assume that we have two database tables in our MySQL database:

- users
- addresses

The **users table** holds data such as your name, e-mail, and password. The **addresses table** holds the addresses belonging to users. Each user can have multiple addresses. So the users and the addresses table are related to each other.

Let's say we want to search for users based on their name and address. The entered search term can be either the name or part of the address. While performing a search directly on the database, our MySQL query would look something like:

```
SELECT u.id, u.name
  FROM users
  AS u LEFT JOIN addresses AS a ON u.id = a.user_id
    WHERE u.name LIKE '%search_term%'
      OR a.address LIKE '%search_term%' GROUP BY u.id;
```

The given query will directly search the specified database tables and get the results. The main advantage of using this approach is that we are always performing a search on the latest version of the available data. Hence, if a new user's data has been inserted just before you initiated the search, you will see that user's data in your search results if it matches your search query.

However, one major disadvantage of this approach is that an SQL query to perform such a search is fired every time a search request comes in, and this becomes an issue when the number of records in the users table increases. With each search query, two tables are joined. This adds overhead and further hinders the performance of the query.

Searching an index

In this approach, a query is not fired directly on a database table. Rather, an index is created from the data stored in the database. This index contains data from all the related tables. The index can itself be stored in a database or on a file system.

The advantage of using this approach is that we need not join tables in SQL queries each time a search request comes in, and the search request would not scan every row stored in the database. The search request is directed towards the index which is highly optimized for searching.

The disadvantage would be the additional storage required to store the index and the time required to build the index. However, these are traded off for the time saved during an actual search request.

Sphinx—a full-text search engine

No, we will not discuss The Great Sphinx of Giza here, we're talking about the other Sphinx, popular in the computing world. Sphinx stands for **SQL Phrase Index**.

Sphinx is a full-text search engine (generally standalone) which provides fast, relevant, efficient full-text search functionality to third-party applications. It was especially created to facilitate searches on SQL databases and integrates very well with scripting languages; such as PHP, Python, Perl, Ruby, and Java.

At the time of writing this book, the latest stable release of Sphinx was v0.9.9.

Features

Some of the major features of Sphinx include (taken from `http://sphinxsearch.com`):

- High indexing speed (up to 10 MB/sec on modern CPUs)
- High search speed (average query is under 0.1 sec on 2 to 4 GB of text collection)
- High scalability (up to 100 GB of text, up to 100 Million documents on a single CPU)
- Supports distributed searching (since v.0.9.6)
- Supports MySQL (MyISAM and InnoDB tables are both supported) and PostgreSQL natively
- Supports phrase searching
- Supports phrase proximity ranking, providing good relevance
- Supports English and Russian stemming
- Supports any number of document fields (weights can be changed on the fly)
- Supports document groups
- Supports **stopwords**, that is, that it indexes only what's most relevant from a given list of words
- Supports different search modes ("match extended", "match all", "match phrase" and "match any" as of v.0.9.5)
- Generic XML interface which greatly simplifies custom integration
- Pure-PHP (that is, NO module compiling and so on) search client API

A brief history

Back in 2001, there weren't many good solutions for searching in web applications. Andrew Aksyonoff, a Russian developer, was facing difficulties in finding a search engine with features such as good search quality (relevance), high searching speed, and low resource requirements - for example, disk usage and CPU.

He tried a few available solutions and even modified them to suit his needs, but in vain. Eventually he decided to come up with his own search engine, which he later named Sphinx.

After the first few releases of Sphinx, Andrew received good feedback from users. Over a period of time, he decided to continue developing Sphinx and founded Sphinx Technologies Inc.

Today Andrew is the primary developer for Sphinx, along with a few others who joined the wagon. At the time of writing, Sphinx was under heavy development, with regular releases.

License

Sphinx is a free and open source software which can be distributed or modified under the terms of the GNU **General Public License (GPL)** as published by the Free Software Foundation, either version 2 or any later version.

However, if you intend to use or embed Sphinx in a project but do not want to disclose the source code as required by GPL, you will need to obtain a commercial license by contacting Sphinx Technologies Inc. at `http://sphinxsearch.com/contacts.html`

Installation

Enough talking, let's get on to some real action. The first step is to install Sphinx itself.

System requirements

Sphinx was developed and tested mostly on UNIX based systems. All modern UNIX based operating systems with an ANSI compliant compiler should be able to compile and run Sphinx without any issues. However, Sphinx has also been found running on the following operating systems without any issues.

- Linux (Kernel 2.4.x and 2.6.x of various distributions)
- Microsoft Windows 2000 and XP
- FreeBSD 4.x, 5.x, 6.x
- NetBSD 1.6, 3.0
- Solaris 9, 11
- Mac OS X

Note: The Windows version of Sphinx is not meant to be used on production servers. It should only be used for testing and debugging. This is the primary reason that all examples given in this book will be for Linux-based systems.

Sphinx on a Unix-based system

If you intend to install Sphinx on a UNIX based system, then you need to check the following:

- C++ compiler (GNU GCC works fine)
- A make program (GNU make works fine)
- The XML libraries libexpat1 (name may be different on non Ubuntu distro) and libexpat1-dev (If you intend to use the xmlpipe2 data source)

Time for action – installation on Linux

1. Download the latest stable version of the sphinx source from `http://sphinxsearch.com/downloads.html`.

2. Extract it anywhere on your file system and go inside the extracted `sphinx` directory:

   ```
   $ tar -xzvf sphinx-0.9.9.tar.gz
   $ cd sphinx-0.9.9
   ```

3. Run the `configure` utility:

   ```
   $ ./configure --prefix=/usr/local/sphinx
   ```

4. Build from the source:

   ```
   $ make
   ```

 It will take a while after you run the `make` command as it builds the binaries from the source code.

5. Install the application (run as root):

   ```
   $ make install
   ```

What just happened?

We downloaded the latest release of Sphinx and extracted it using the `tar` command. We then ran the `configure` command which gets the details of our machine and also checks for all dependencies. If any of the dependency is missing, it will throw an error. We will take a look at possible dependency issues in a while.

Once we are done with `configure`, the `make` command will build (compile) the source code. After that, `make install` will actually install the binaries to respective location as specified in `--prefix` option to the `configure`.

Options to the configure command

There are many options that can be passed to the `configure` command but we will take a look at a few important ones:

- `--prefix=/path`: This option specifies the path to install the sphinx binaries. In this book it is assumed that sphinx was configured with `--prefix=/usr/local/sphinx` so it is recommended that you configure your path with the same prefix.

- `--with-mysql=/path`: Sphinx needs to know where to find MySQL's include and library files. It auto-detects this most of the time but if for any reason it fails, you can supply the path here.

- `--with-pgsql=/path`: Same as `--with-mysql` but for PostgreSQL.

Most of the common errors you would find while configuring sphinx are related to missing MySQL include files.

```
configuring Sphinx
------------------

checking for CFLAGS needed for pthreads... none
checking for LIBS needed for pthreads... -lpthread
checking for pthreads... found
checking whether to compile with MySQL support... yes
checking for mysql_config... not found
checking MySQL include files... configure: error: missing include files.

********************************************************************************
ERROR: cannot find MySQL include files.

Check that you do have MySQL include files installed.
The package name is typically 'mysql-devel'.

If include files are installed on your system, but you are still getting
this message, you should do one of the following:

1) either specify includes location explicitly, using --with-mysql-includes;
2) or specify MySQL installation root location explicitly, using --with-mysql;
3) or make sure that the path to 'mysql_config' program is listed in
   your PATH environment variable.

To disable MySQL support, use --without-mysql option.
********************************************************************************
```

This can be caused either because Sphinx's auto detection for MySQL include path failed, or MySQL's devel package has not been installed on your machine. If MySQL's devel package is not installed, you can install it using the Software Package Manager (apt or yum) of your operating system. In case of Ubuntu, the package is called `libmysqlclient16-dev`.

 If you intend to use Sphinx without MySQL then you can use the configure option `--without-mysql`.

You need to follow pretty much the same steps if PostgreSQL include files are missing. In this book we will be primarily using MySQL for all examples.

Known issues during installation

Listed next are a few errors or issues that may arise during Sphinx's installation make can sometimes fail with the following error:

```
/bin/sh: g++: command not found
make[1]: *** [libsphinx_a-sphinx.o] Error 127
```

This may be because of a missing `gcc-c++` package. Try installing it.

At times you might get compile-time errors like:

```
sphinx.cpp:67: error: invalid application of `sizeof' to
    incomplete type `Private::SizeError<false>'
```

To fix the above error try editing `sphinx.h` and replace `off_t` with `DWORD` in a `typedef` for `SphOffset_t`.

```
#define STDOUT_FILENO             fileno(stdout)
#else
typedef DWORD                     SphOffset_t;
#endif
```

One drawback of doing this would be that you won't be able to use full-text indexes larger than 2 GB.

Sphinx on Windows

Installing on a Windows system is easier than on a Linux system as you can use the pre-compiled binaries.

Time for action – installation on Windows

1. Download the Win32 binaries of Sphinx from `http://www.sphinxsearch.com/downloads.html`. Choose the binary depending on whether you want MySQL support, or PostgreSQL support, or both.

2. Extract the downloaded ZIP to any suitable location. Let's assume it is extracted to `C:\>sphinx`.

3. Install the searched system as a Windows service by issuing the following command in the Command Prompt:

```
C:\sphinx\bin\searchd -install -config C:\sphinx\sphinx.conf -
servicename SphinxSearch
```

This will install `searchd` as a service but it won't be started yet. Before starting the Sphinx service we need to create the `sphinx.conf` file and create indexes. This will be done in the next few chapters.

What just happened?

Installing Sphinx on windows is a straight-forward task. We have pre-compiled binaries for the windows platform, which can be used directly.

After extracting the ZIP, we installed the Sphinx service. We need not install anything else since binaries for `indexer` and search are readily available in the `C:\sphinx\bin` directory.

The use of binaries to create indexes and the use of the searchd service to search will be covered in the next few chapters.

At the time of writing this book, the Windows version of Sphinx is not meant to be used in production environment. It is highly recommended to use the Linux version of Sphinx in your production environment.

Sphinx on Mac OS X

Installation on a Mac is very similar to how it is done on Linux systems. You need to build it from source and then install the generated binaries.

Time for action – installation on a Mac

1. Download the latest stable version of the sphinx source from
`http://sphinxsearch.com/downloads.html`.

```
$ tar -xzvf sphinx-0.9.9.tar.gz
$ cd sphinx-0.9.9
```

2. Run the configure utility:

```
$ ./configure -prefix=/usr/local/sphinx
```

3. If you are on a 64 bit Mac then use the following command to configure:

```
LDFLAGS="-arch x86_64" ./configure --prefix=/usr/local/sphinx
$ make
$ sudo make install
```

4. Next, run the make command:

```
$ make
```

5. Finally, run the following command to complete your configuration:

```
$ sudo make install
```

What just happened?

We downloaded the Sphinx source and extracted it using the tar command. We then configured Sphinx and built it using the make command. The options to configure are the same as we used while installing Sphinx in Linux.

The only notable difference between installation on Linux and Mac is that if your Mac is 64 bit, your configure command is changed slightly as given above.

Other supported systems

Above we learned how to install Sphinx on Linux, Windows, and Mac. However, these are not the only systems on which Sphinx can be installed. Sphinx is also supported on the following systems:

- FreeBSD 4.x, 5.x, 6.x
- NetBSD 1.6, 3.0
- Solaris 9, 11

 Installation procedure for the above mentioned systems is more or less similar to how it is done on a Linux system.

Summary

In this chapter:

- ◆ We saw the different ways to perform search
- ◆ We got to know about Sphinx and how it helps in performing searches
- ◆ We took a look at some of Sphinx's features and its brief history
- ◆ We learned how to install Sphinx on different operating systems

By now you should have installed Sphinx on your system and laid the foundation for *Chapter 2, Getting Started*, where we will get started with Sphinx and some basic usage.

2
Getting Started

Now that we have installed Sphinx, let's move forward and take a look at different search techniques and get acquainted with the different utilities Sphinx has to offer.

In this chapter we will take a dive into full-text search and look at different advantages of it. We will then see how Sphinx utilizes full-text search and also learn about indexer, search *and* searchd *utilities that come along with Sphinx. We will also see a very basic example of how Sphinx works.*

 Make sure that you have installed Sphinx using the steps mentioned in *Chapter 1, Setting Up Sphinx* before proceeding.

Checking the installation

Before we proceed any further, let's first check whether Sphinx was properly installed on our system. As we had used the --prefix configure option during installation, all Sphinx binaries and configuration files must have been placed in one single directory, that is, the one which was specified with --prefix.

We are assuming that you have installed Sphinx on a Linux machine. If everything went fine then a directory /usr/local/sphinx should have been created on your system. It should be structured in the same way as the following screenshot.

I have used a Linux (Ubuntu 10.04) machine for all the examples shown in this book. Further, I presume that you have installed Sphinx with the configure option `--prefix=/usr/local/sphinx`

```
abbas@abbas:/usr/local/sphinx$ tree
.
|-- bin
|   |-- indexer
|   |-- indextool
|   |-- search
|   |-- searchd
|    `-- spelldump
|-- etc
|   |-- example.sql
|   |-- sphinx.conf.dist
|    `-- sphinx-min.conf.dist
 `-- var
    |-- data
     `-- log

5 directories, 8 files
```

You can see that we have a few binary files in `bin` directory and few configuration files in the `etc` directory. Then we have the `var` directory that will hold the actual index data and search logs. We will look at all of these in details in later chapters.

To test whether the Sphinx binary is working first change your directory to `bin`:

$ cd /usr/local/sphinx/bin

Then issue the command`./indexer`:

```
abbas@abbas:/usr/local/sphinx/bin$ ./indexer
Sphinx 0.9.9-release (r2117)
Copyright (c) 2001-2009, Andrew Aksyonoff

Usage: indexer [OPTIONS] [indexname1 [indexname2 [...]]]

Options are:
--config <file>         read configuration from specified file
                        (default is sphinx.conf)
--all                   reindex all configured indexes
--quiet                 be quiet, only print errors
--noprogress            do not display progress
                        (automatically on if output is not to a tty)
```

You can see that it outputs some information along with the version of Sphinx being installed, which in our case is 0.9.9.

The output above confirms that we are good to go, so let's move forward

Full-text search

Sphinx is a full-text search engine. So, before going any further, we need to understand what full-text search is and how it excels over the traditional searching.

What is full-text search?

Full-text search is one of the techniques for searching a document or database stored on a computer. While searching, the search engine goes through and examines all of the words stored in the document and tries to match the search query against those words. A complete examination of all the words (text) stored in the document is undertaken and hence it is called a full-text search.

Full-text search excels in searching large volumes of unstructured text quickly and effectively. It returns pages based on how well they match the user's query.

Traditional search

To understand the difference between a normal search and full-text search, let's take an example of a MySQL database table and perform searches on it.

It is assumed that MySQL Server and phpMyAdmin are already installed on your system.

Time for action – normal search in MySQL

1. Open phpMyAdmin in your browser and create a new database called **myblog**.

2. Select the **myblog** database:

3. Create a table by executing the following query:

```
CREATE TABLE `posts` (
`id` INT NOT NULL AUTO_INCREMENT PRIMARY KEY ,
`title` VARCHAR( 255 ) NOT NULL ,
`description` TEXT NOT NULL ,
`created` DATETIME NOT NULL ,
`modified` DATETIME NOT NULL
) ENGINE = MYISAM;
```

 Queries can be executed from the **SQL** page in phpMyAdmin. You can find the link to that page in the top menu.

4. Populate the table with some records:

```
INSERT INTO `posts`(`id`, `title`, `description`, `created`,
`modified`) VALUES
(1, 'PHP scripting language', 'PHP is a web scripting language
originally created by Rasmus Lerdorf', NOW(), NOW()),
(2, 'Programming Languages', 'There are many languages available
to cater any kind of programming need', NOW(), NOW()),
(3, 'My Life', 'This post is about my life which in a sense is
beautiful', NOW(), NOW()),
(4, 'Life on Mars', 'Is there any life on mars?', NOW(), NOW());
```

5. Next, run the following queries against the table:

```
SELECT * FROM posts WHERE title LIKE 'programming%';
```

id	title	description	
2	Programming Languages	There are many languages available to cater any ki...	2

The above query returns row **2**.

```
SELECT * FROM posts WHERE description LIKE '%life%';
```

id	title	description	created
3	My Life	This post is about my life which in a sense is bea...	2010-07-21 10:22:
4	Life on Mars	Is there any life on mars?	2010-07-21 10:22:

The above query return rows **3** and **4**.

```
SELECT * FROM posts WHERE description LIKE '%scripting language%';
```

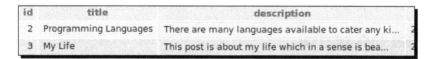

The above query returns row **1**.

```
SELECT * FROM posts WHERE description LIKE '%beautiful%' OR
description LIKE '%programming%';
```

id	title	description	
2	Programming Languages	There are many languages available to cater any ki...	2
3	My Life	This post is about my life which in a sense is bea...	2

The above query returns rows **2** and **3**.

phpMyAdmin

To administer MySQL database, I highly recommend using a GUI interface tool like phpMyAdmin (`http://www.phpmyadmin.net`). All the above mentioned queries can easily be executed in phpMyAdmin and the results are displayed in a user friendly manner.

What just happened?

We first created a table `posts` to hold some data. Each post has a `title` and a `description`. We then populated the table with some records.

With the first `SELECT` query we tried to find all posts where the `title` starts with the word **programming**. This correctly gave us the row number **2**. But what if you want to search for the word anywhere in the field and not just at that start? For this we fired the second query, wherein we searched for the word **life** anywhere in the description of the post. Again this worked pretty well for us and as expected we got the result in the form of row numbers **3** and **4**.

Now what if we wanted to search for multiple words? For this we fired the third query where we searched for the words **scripting language**. As row **1** has those words in its `description`, it was returned correctly.

Until now everything looked fine and we were able to perform searches without any hassle. The query gets complex when we want to search for multiple words and those words are not necessarily placed consecutively in a field, that is, side by side. One such example is shown in the form of our fourth query where we tried to search for the words **programming** and **beautiful** in the description of the posts. Since the number of words we need to search for increases, this query gets complicated, and moreover, slow in execution, since it needs to match each word individually.

The previous SELECT queries and their output also don't give us any information about the relevance of the search terms with the results found. **Relevance** can be defined as a measure of how closely the returned database records match the user's search query. In other words, how pertinent the result set is to the search query.

Relevance is very important in the search world because users want to see the items with highest relevance at the top of their search results. One of the major reasons for the success of Google is that their search results are always sorted by relevance.

MySQL full-text search

This is where full-text search comes to the rescue. MySQL has inbuilt support for full-text search and you only need to add FULLTEXT INDEX to the field against which you want to perform your search.

Continuing the earlier example of the posts table, let's add a full-text index to the description field of the table. Run the following query:

```
ALTER TABLE `posts` ADD FULLTEXT (
`description`
);
```

The query will add an **INDEX** of type **FULLTEXT** to the description field of the posts table.

 Only MyISAM Engine in MySQL supports the full-text indexes.

Now to search for all the records which contain the words **programming** or **beautiful** anywhere in their description, the query would be:

```
SELECT * FROM posts WHERE
  MATCH (description) AGAINST ('beautiful programming');
```

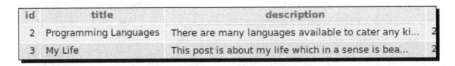

id	title	description	
2	Programming Languages	There are many languages available to cater any ki...	2
3	My Life	This post is about my life which in a sense is bea...	2

This query will return rows **2** and **3**, and the returned results are sorted by relevance. One more thing to note is that this query takes less time than the earlier query, which used **LIKE** for matching.

By default, the MATCH() function performs a natural language search, it attempts to use natural language processing to understand the nature of the query and then search accordingly.

Full-text search in MySQL is a big topic in itself and we have only seen the tip of the iceberg. For a complete reference, please refer to the MySQL manual at `http://dev.mysql.com/doc/`.

Advantages of full-text search

The following points are some of the major advantages of full-text search:

- It is quicker than traditional searches as it benefits from an index of words that is used to look up records instead of doing a full table scan
- It gives results that can be sorted by relevance to the searched phrase or term, with sophisticated ranking capabilities to find the best documents or records
- It performs very well on huge databases with millions of records
- It skips the common words such as the, an, for, and so on

When to use a full-text search?

- When there is a high volume of free-form text data to be searched
- When there is a need for highly optimized search results
- When there is a demand for flexible search querying

Overview of Sphinx

Sphinx is an external solution for database search, which means that it runs outside the main database used for your application. It takes data from the database and creates indexes that are stored on a file system. These indexes are highly optimized for searching and your application uses an API to search the indexes.

Sphinx interacts with the database using a data source driver which comes along with Sphinx. You need to specify which data source driver should be used by Sphinx in its configuration file.

Primary programs

As shown at the beginning of this chapter, Sphinx is shipped with some binary programs which were installed at `/usr/local/sphinx/bin` directory. Let's take a look at two principal programs that are used by Sphinx for indexing and searching purposes.

- **indexer**: This program is used for indexing and re-indexing full-text indexes. By default, Sphinx reads the configuration file at `/usr/local/sphinx/etc/sphinx.conf` to know what and how to index. We will be dealing with `sphinx.conf` in more detail during later chapters.

◆ **searchd**: This is the daemon used for searching the indexes. It requires a client to access the Sphinx API. There are a number of `searchd` client API implementations available for Sphinx.

Enough talking about Sphinx, now let's see it in action...

Time for action – Sphinx in action

Let's see an example of how Sphinx works. We will create an index and then search it using the Sphinx command line utility as well as the PHP client implementation. So let's begin:

1. Firstly, create a MySQL database named **test**, if it is not already there:

```
CREATE DATABASE test;
```

Sphinx ships with a sample configuration file and a sample database table to be used for demo purposes. The SQL for the table is located at `/usr/local/sphinx/etc/example.sql` and it contains the following SQL:

```
DROP TABLE IF EXISTS test.documents;

CREATE TABLE test.documents
(
  id  INTEGER PRIMARY KEY NOT NULL AUTO_INCREMENT,
  group_id  INTEGER NOT NULL,
  group_id2  INTEGER NOT NULL,
  date_added  DATETIME NOT NULL,
  title  VARCHAR(255) NOT NULL,
  content  TEXT NOT NULL
);

REPLACE INTO test.documents ( id, group_id, group_id2, date_added,
title, content ) VALUES
  ( 1, 1, 5, NOW(), 'test one', 'this is my test document number
one. also checking search within phrases.' ),
  ( 2, 1, 6, NOW(), 'test two', 'this is my test document number
two' ),
  ( 3, 2, 7, NOW(), 'another doc', 'this is another group' ),
  ( 4, 2, 8, NOW(), 'doc number four', 'this is to test groups'
);

DROP TABLE IF EXISTS test.tags;

CREATE TABLE test.tags
(
  docid INTEGER NOT NULL,
```

```
    tagid INTEGER NOT NULL,
    UNIQUE(docid,tagid)
);

INSERT INTO test.tags VALUES
    (1,1), (1,3), (1,5), (1,7),
    (2,6), (2,4), (2,2),
    (3,15),
    (4,7), (4,40);
```

You can copy the SQL and paste it in your phpMyAdmin interface to run the SQL or execute the following command to import the SQL from the command line in Linux:

```
$ mysql -u root < /usr/local/sphinx/etc/example.sql
```

2. Next, create the configuration file (you may need the permissions to create the file):

```
$ cd /usr/local/sphinx/etc
$ cp sphinx-min.conf.dist sphinx.conf
```

Now edit sphinx.conf in your favorite editor (you may need to change the permissions of the file to be able to modify it).

The first block of the file looks something like this:

```
source src1
{
  type          = mysql

  sql_host      = localhost
  sql_user      = test
  sql_pass      =
  sql_db        = test
  sql_port      = 3306   # optional, default is 3306

  sql_query     = \
    SELECT id, group_id, UNIX_TIMESTAMP(date_added) \
      AS date_added, title, content \
    FROM documents

  sql_attr_uint       = group_id
  sql_attr_timestamp  = date_added

  sql_query_info      = SELECT * FROM documents WHERE id=$id
}
```

3. Change the value of **sql_host**, **sql_user**, **sql_pass** and **sql_db** as per your system:

```
sql_host        = localhost
sql_user        = myuser
sql_pass        = mypass
sql_db          = test
```

If you have not installed the Sphinx at `/usr/local/sphinx` then you will need to modify the paths of the following options as well:

- ❑ path
- ❑ log
- ❑ query_log
- ❑ pid_file

4. Now run the `indexer`:

```
$ /usr/local/sphinx/bin/indexer --all
```

This will give output as shown in the following screenshot

```
Sphinx 0.9.9-release (r2117)
Copyright (c) 2001-2009, Andrew Aksyonoff

using config file '/usr/local/sphinx/etc/sphinx.conf'...
indexing index 'test1'...
collected 4 docs, 0.0 MB
sorted 0.0 Mhits, 100.0% done
total 4 docs, 193 bytes
total 0.034 sec, 5561 bytes/sec, 115.26 docs/sec
total 2 reads, 0.000 sec, 0.1 kb/call avg, 0.0 msec/call avg
total 7 writes, 0.000 sec, 0.1 kb/call avg, 0.0 msec/call avg
```

If you have installed Sphinx at a location other than `/usr/local/sphinx`, then you need to use the `-c /path/to/sphinx.conf` option in the previous command.

5. Next, let's query the index to see if it works:

```
$ /usr/local/sphinx/bin/search test
```

```
displaying matches:
1. document=1, weight=2, group_id=1, date_added=Thu Jul 22 17:26:25 2010
        id=1
        group_id=1
        group_id2=5
        date_added=2010-07-22 17:26:25
        title=test one
        content=this is my test document number one. also checking search w
2. document=2, weight=2, group_id=1, date_added=Thu Jul 22 17:26:25 2010
        id=2
        group_id=1
        group_id2=6
        date_added=2010-07-22 17:26:25
        title=test two
        content=this is my test document number two
3. document=4, weight=1, group_id=2, date_added=Thu Jul 22 17:26:25 2010
        id=4
        group_id=2
        group_id2=8
        date_added=2010-07-22 17:26:25
        title=doc number four
        content=this is to test groups

words:
1. 'test': 3 documents, 5 hits
```

To query the index from our PHP scripts, we first need to start the **searchd** daemon

```
$ /usr/local/sphinx/bin/searchd
```

```
using config file '/usr/local/sphinx/etc/sphinx.conf'...
listening on all interfaces, port=9312
```

To run `searchd` commands, you need to be the `root` user. You can either switch to root user using the `su` - command, or you could prefix all `searchd` commands with `sudo`.

6. Now, go to the directory where you extracted the Sphinx tarball during installation (in *Chapter 1, Setting Up Sphinx*) and run the command as shown here:

```
$ cd /path/to/sphinx-0.9.9
```

```
$ php api/test.php test
```

The command will output the search results, which confirms that **searchd** is working properly and we can search from our applications using the client API.

```
Query 'test ' retrieved 3 of 3 matches in 0.001 sec.
Query stats:
    'test' found 5 times in 3 documents

Matches:
1. doc_id=1, weight=101, group_id=1, date_added=2010-07-22 17:26:25
2. doc_id=2, weight=101, group_id=1, date_added=2010-07-22 17:26:25
3. doc_id=4, weight=1, group_id=2, date_added=2010-07-22 17:26:25
```

What just happened?

We created an index from the data stored in a MySQL table. We then used Sphinx's **search** utility to search for the **test** term in the index. The results showed that Sphinx is working properly and that the index we created was fine.

The major difference between search results by MySQL and Sphinx is that Sphinx does not return the actual data but only the document id. Using these document IDs, we need to fetch the actual data (from its source) to display it. Along with the document id, Sphinx also returns all the **attributes** and **weight** of each document. The higher the weight, the higher the relevance of that document with the search query.

We then used the PHP implementation of the Sphinx Client API to search for the same **test** term, but this time from within a PHP script.

Data to be indexed

The first thing we did was to create a MySQL database and then import the sample data in to it. This gave us the data as shown in the following screenshot:

id	group_id	group_id2	date_added	title	content
1	1	5	2010-07-22 17:26:25	test one	this is my test document number one. also chec phrases.
2	1	6	2010-07-22 17:26:25	test two	this is my test document number two
3	2	7	2010-07-22 17:26:25	another doc	this is another group
4	2	8	2010-07-22 17:26:25	doc number four	this is to test groups

 Throughout this book, the dates and times shown may differ from what you would have in your database or index. So don't worry about that.

Creating the Sphinx configuration file

Sphinx creates an index based on the options defined in the Sphinx configuration file **sphinx. conf**. This file is divided into different sections:

- ◆ **source**: This section holds all the settings related to the source of the data to be indexed, which in our case is a MySQL database.
- ◆ **index**: This section holds options which tell Sphinx where and how to save the index. These options are used during indexing-time.
- ◆ **indexer**: This section holds options for the `indexer` program.
- ◆ **searchd**: This section holds the options used while searching the index.

In this chapter we will not go into great detail about all the options used in the configuration file. However, a few options to look for are:

- ◆ **sql_***: These options are there to tell Sphinx about different MySQL settings; such as username, password, the database to use, and the port to use.
- ◆ **sql_query**: This option holds the query that will be fired in order to get the data from the MySQL database.

Once the configuration file is ready, index can be created by issuing the following command.

```
$ /usr/local/sphinx/bin/indexer –all
```

During the indexing operation, some information is displayed in the console such as what configuration file is being used by the `indexer`, how many documents were found, how much time it took to index, and other related information.

> To run `indexer` commands, you need to be the root user. You can either switch to root user using the `su` - command, or you could prefix all `indexer` commands with `sudo`.

Searching the index

Sphinx provides a command-line utility search which comes in handy to quickly query the index that we created earlier. However, this utility should only be used for testing purposes. In the production environment one should always use the searchd and its client API implementation.

```
$ /usr/local/sphinx/bin/search test
```

The output of the search command gives us the results that matched the search term **test**. The result shows us the document `id` and weight, amongst other information for the queried term.

Similar information is displayed when we use the PHP client API to search.

Have a go hero

We created a very basic example to see how Sphinx works; however, you can extend and explore this by:

- Adding a few more records to the **documents** table
- Re-indexing the **documents** table
- Searching with different search phrases and examining the returned results and their weights

Why use Sphinx for full-text searching?

If you're looking for a good **Database Management System** (**DBMS**), there are plenty of options available with support for full-text indexing and searches, such as MySQL, PostgreSQL, and SQL Server. There are also external full-text search engines, such as Lucene and Solr. Let's see the advantages of using Sphinx over the DBMS's full-text searching capabilities and other external search engines:

- It has a higher indexing speed. It is 50 to 100 times faster than MySQL FULLTEXT and 4 to 10 times faster than other external search engines.
- It also has higher searching speed since it depends heavily on the mode, Boolean vs. phrase, and additional processing. It is up to 500 times faster than MySQL FULLTEXT in cases involving a large result set with GROUP BY. It is more than two times faster in searching than other external search engines available.
- As mentioned earlier, relevancy is among the key features one expects when using a search engine, and Sphinx performs very well in this area. It has phrase-based ranking in addition to classic statistical BM25 ranking.
- Last but not the least, Sphinx has better scalability. It can be scaled vertically (utilizing many CPUs, many HDDs) or horizontally (utilizing many servers), and this comes out of the box with Sphinx. One of the biggest known Sphinx cluster has over 3 billion records with more than 2 terabytes of size.

In one of his presentations, Andrew Aksyonoff (creator of Sphinx) presented the following benchmarking results. Approximately 3.5 Million records with around 5 GB of text were used for the purpose.

	MySQL	Lucene	Sphinx
Indexing time, min	1627	176	84
Index size, MB	3011	6328	2850
Match all, ms/q	286	30	22
Match phrase, ms/q	3692	29	21
Match bool top-20, ms/q	24	29	13

Apart from a basic search, there are many features that make Sphinx a better solution for searching. These features include multivalve attributes, tokenizing settings, wordforms, HTML processing, geosearching, ranking, and many others. We will be taking a more elaborate look at some of these features in later chapters.

Summary

In this chapter:

- We learned how to check whether Sphinx was installed properly or not. We saw the directory structure Sphinx creates to store its binary files, configuration files, and other data.

- We then learned what full-text search is and what its advantages over normal search are. We also saw how full-text search has been implemented in MySQL with an example. We saw the syntax of an SQL query used to search a full-text indexed field in MySQL.

- We have also seen why to use Sphinx, an external search engine, instead of database's native full-text support. We saw how Sphinx excels in many ways, and outperforms most of the databases and external search engines available today.

- Lastly we saw how to create an index using the `indexer` utility, and then how to search that index from the command line as well as other applications using client API implementations.

Having armed ourselves with all the basics we need to know, we are ready to start creating indexes with more options available to us.

3
Indexing

This chapter is all about indexes and how to create them in Sphinx. Indexes are the most important component when using Sphinx.

In this chapter we shall:

♦ See what indexes are and how they help in searching. We will also learn how they are created by using Sphinx's `indexer` utility.

♦ We will learn what data sources are and what different types are available in Sphinx.

So let's get on with it...

What are indexes?

Wikipedia defines a database index as follows:

> *A database index is a data structure that improves the speed of data retrieval operations on a database table at the cost of slower writes and increased storage space.*

Let's use an example to understand this. A library has a catalog of all the books at its disposal. If you want to look for a particular book, you will quickly search through the catalog instead of searching through every isle or shelf for that book. The catalog acts as an index of all the books.

In the computing world an index is something similar. It saves you the trouble of having to search through every record in the database. Instead, you speed up your query by searching a subset of data that is highly optimized for quick reference. This set of data is called an **index** and it is separate from the original data stored in the database.

To give you a better picture of this, the following table relates a *Library* to a *Database*.

Library	Database
Library is a collection of books	Database is a collection of data
To find a book, you go through every row of the shelves	To find a match, you go through every record in the database table
To facilitate searching, a library maintains a catalog	To facilitate searching, a database maintains indexes
It is easy to refer to a catalog to figure out where to find a book	It is easy to refer to an index to find out a record
When a new book is added, the librarian has to update the catalog	When a new record is inserted, the index has to be updated

The drawback of creating an index is that it requires additional space to store the index and additional time to create it as well. However, the speed we gain while searching overshadows these drawbacks by miles.

Indexes in Sphinx

Indexes in Sphinx are a bit different from indexes we have in databases. The data that Sphinx indexes is a set of structured **documents** and each document has the same set of fields. This is very similar to SQL, where each row in the table corresponds to a document and each column to a field.

Sphinx builds a special data structure that is optimized for answering full-text search queries. This structure is called an **index** and the process of creating an index from the data is called **indexing**.

The indexes in Sphinx can also contain attributes that are highly optimized for filtering. These attributes are not full-text indexed and do not contribute to matching. However, they are very useful at filtering out the results we want based on attribute values.

There can be different types of indexes suited for different tasks. The index type, which has been implemented in Sphinx, is designed for maximum indexing and searching speed.

The indexes are stored in a file on the file system as specified in the Sphinx configuration file. In the previous chapter it was `/usr/local/sphinx/var/data/test1`.

Index attributes

Attributes in an index are used to perform additional filtering and sorting during search. They are basically additional values linked to each document in the index.

Let's try to understand the attributes using an example. Suppose you want to search through a catalog of books stored in the index. You want the results to be sorted by the date on which the book was published and then by the cost of the book. For this you need not put the date and cost of the book in the full-text index. You can specify these two values as attributes and then sort the results of you search query by these attributes. These attributes will play no role in searching but will play a major role in sorting the search results.

 Attributes play some role in relevancy when SPH_SORT _EXPR sort mode is used

Another use of attributes would be to filter the search results. You can filter your results for the specified date range so that only those books that were published in the given time period are returned.

Another good example to understand the attributes would be a blogging system. Typically only the title and content of a blog post needs to be full-text searchable, despite the fact that on many occasions we want the search to be limited to a certain author or category. For such cases we can use attributes to filter the search results, and we can return only those posts whose author (or category) attribute in the index is the same as the selected author or category filter.

So, full-text search results can not only be processed based on matching documents, but on many other document attributes as well. It is possible to sort the results purely based on attributes.

One other important characteristic of attributes is that they are returned in search results while the actual indexed data is not. When displaying search results, you may use the returned attribute values as it is, while for displaying the full-text data you need to get it from the original source.

Types of attributes

The data on the basis of which the documents should be filtered can be of various types. To cater to this and for more efficient filtering, attributes can be of the following types:

- Unsigned integers (1 bit to 32 bit wide)
- Floating point values (32 bit, IEEE 754 single precision)
- String ordinals --enable-id64

- ◆ UNIX timestamps
- ◆ **Multi-value attributes (MVA)**

Attribute names are always case insensitive. They are stored in the index but cannot be searched as full-text.

Multi-value attributes (MVA)

MVAs are a special type of attribute in Sphinx that make it possible to attach multiple values to every document. These attributes are especially useful in cases where each document can have multiple values for the same property (field).

In our previous example of a blog post, each post can have multiple tags associated with it. Now if you want to filter the search based on tags, MVAs can be used in this case. For example, a post has *php*, *programming,* and *opensource* as tags, and if we use an MVA to hold these values, then filtering a search by any of those three tags would return the same post (and any other posts with the same tags).

MVAs are specified as lists and its entries are limited to unsigned 32-bit integers. The list itself is not limited and an MVA can hold any number of entries for each document, as long as RAM permits.

 Search results can be filtered or grouped by MVA but cannot be sorted by MVA.

Data sources

The source of the data that is to be indexed is called a **data source**. The data can generally come from very different sources such as SQL databases, plain text files, HTML documents, web services, mailboxes, and so on.

Sphinx cannot directly connect to a data source and fetch the required data. For different sources Sphinx requires different code to prepare the data for indexing. The code that does this job is called as **data source driver** (or data source for brevity).

Sphinx is available with pre-built data source drivers for MySQL and PostgreSQL databases. These drivers can connect to the database using Sphinx's native C/C++ API to run queries and fetch the data. The retrieved data is then indexed and stored in the indexes.

Another driver called **xmlpipe2** (and **xmlpipe** which is now deprecated) is shipped with Sphinx. This driver executes the specified command and reads the data from its `stdout`. The data is expected in a predefined XML structure. This data source is very useful when indexing data from non-conventional sources such as mailboxes, web service, plain text files, and so on. This data source can also be used to get the data from a database.

Data sources are defined in Sphinx configuration files and there can be multiple sources per index. Multiple sources are processed sequentially in the very same order in which they were specified in the index definition. The data (thus documents) from all the sources are merged as if they were coming from a single source.

In this book we will be going through the following data sources in detail:

- ◆ MySQL data source
- ◆ xmlpipe data source

How to define the data source?

Data sources are defined in the Sphinx configuration file (in our case `/usr/local/sphinx/etc/sphinx.conf`). The data source block looks something like:

```
source name
{
  # Source options
  type = mysql
  ....... .
  ....... .
}
```

We need to provide a name to each source followed by the source options. The **type** option specifies whether the data source is MySQL or PostgreSQL, or xmlpipe or xmlpipe2. We will be looking at the respective data source options, which are dependent on the `type`, later in the chapter.

SQL data sources

As mentioned earlier, Sphinx ships with two SQL data sources: MySQL and PostgreSQL. Let's see how we can use these data sources to create indexes that can later be searched using the **searchd** daemon.

 All our examples will use MySQL as the source database. However, there shouldn't be any major difference in defining a source for PostgreSQL.

Let's start by understanding how the MySQL data source worked in the example we saw in *Chapter 2, Getting Started*.

The data source configuration was as given next:

```
source src1
{
  type           = mysql

  sql_host       = localhost
  sql_user       = test
  sql_pass       =
  sql_db         = test
  sql_port       = 3306        # optional, default is 3306

  sql_query      = \
    SELECT id, group_id, UNIX_TIMESTAMP(date_added) AS date_added,
title, content \
    FROM documents

  sql_attr_uint       = group_id
  sql_attr_timestamp    = date_added

  sql_query_info       = SELECT * FROM documents WHERE id=$id
}
```

In this case we named the data source as `src1`. We specified that we will be using MySQL as the source database with the help of the `type` option.

The next few options like `sql_host`, `sql_user`, `sql_pass`, `sql_db` and `sql_port` were used to define the connection parameters for connecting to the MySQL database.

Now let's understand what `sql_query` is used for. This option is used to specify the main SQL query that will fetch the data from the database. This is a mandatory option if you are using an SQL data source and there can only be one main query per source.

Select as many fields in the query as you want to be included in the index. However, document ID must be the very first field and it **must be a unique unsigned positive integer**. In this case the `id` field of the `documents` table will be treated as **document id** in the created index.

Document ID should be the first field in the SQL query and it must be a unique unsigned non-zero, non-negative integer number. If you are using multiple sources for an index then the document IDs must be unique across all sources.

All the fields (except document ID) selected by the query are, by default, treated as full-text fields in the created index. If you want one or more fields to act as attributes in the index then you can do so with the help of the sql_attr_* option. In the previous example, we declared group_id to be an attribute of type unsigned integer and date_added to be an attribute of type timestamp. The following options can be used to declare different types of attributes:

♦ sql_attr_unit: Unsigned integer attribute (32 bit)

♦ sql_attr_bool: Boolean attribute

♦ sql_attr_bigint: Signed integer attribute (64 bit)

♦ sql_attr_timestamp: Unix timestamp attribute

♦ sql_attr_str2ordinal: Ordinal string number attribute

♦ sql_attr_float: Floating point attribute

♦ sql_attr_multi: Multi-valued attribute (MVA)

As we had inserted four rows in the documents table, the query will retrieve all the four rows and create the index with id as document id, title and content as full-text fields, group_id as an unsigned integer attribute, and date_added as timestamp attribute.

When a search is performed on the index, the search term is matched against title and content fields, while the two attributes can be used for sorting and filtering.

The last option in the source configuration is sql_query_info and this is optional. This option only applies to MySQL source type. It is used by the CLI **search** utility to fetch and display document information. The **$id** macro is required and it expands to the queried document ID. By default the CLI search utility will display only the attributes stored in the index for the matched documents. If you want to display the actual text that was full-text indexed or any other information related to the matched document, the sql_query_info option comes in handy.

Creating Index using SQL data source (Blog)

Now let's take a look at how to create indexes using a MySQL data source. We will understand this with the help of a small blogging application.

We are going to assume that our blogging application has some frontend to manage the posts, authors, and categories. We will only deal with the database part of it.

We will assume that each blog post is written by one author and it can be assigned multiple categories. Also, the same category can be assigned to multiple blog posts.

Our aim is to create an index for blog posts that can be searched from within our application. We will create indexes in steps, and our first step would be to create a simple index with only full-text indexed fields and no attributes. Next we will try to add simple attributes so that search can be filtered based on authors and date. Lastly we will try our hand at multi-value attributes (MVAs) and see what configuration options to use in order to add them to the index.

Creating a simple index without any attributes

Let's create an index that would essentially work in a very similar way to the database table itself. It will have two full-text indexed fields: title and content.

Time for action – creating database tables for a blog

1. Create the database by executing the following query:

   ```
   CREATE DATABASE myblog
   ```

2. Create the posts table:

   ```
   CREATE TABLE `myblog`.`posts` (
   `id` INT UNSIGNED NOT NULL AUTO_INCREMENT PRIMARY KEY ,
   `title` VARCHAR( 255 ) NOT NULL ,
   `content` TEXT NOT NULL ,
   `author_id` INT UNSIGNED NOT NULL ,
   `publish_date` DATETIME NOT NULL
   ) ENGINE = MYISAM;
   ```

3. Create the authors table:

   ```
   CREATE TABLE `myblog`.`authors` (
   `id` INT UNSIGNED NOT NULL AUTO_INCREMENT PRIMARY KEY ,
   `name` VARCHAR( 50 ) NOT NULL
   ) ENGINE = MYISAM;
   ```

4. Create the categories table:

   ```
   CREATE TABLE `myblog`.`categories` (
   `id` INT UNSIGNED NOT NULL AUTO_INCREMENT PRIMARY KEY ,
   `name` VARCHAR( 50 ) NOT NULL
   ) ENGINE = MYISAM;
   ```

5. Create the `posts_categories` table:

```
CREATE TABLE `myblog`.`posts_categories` (
`post_id` INT UNSIGNED NOT NULL ,
`category_id` INT UNSIGNED NOT NULL ,
PRIMARY KEY ( `post_id` , `category_id` )
) ENGINE = MYISAM;
```

What just happened?

We created a database to hold the tables needed for our blog application. We then created the following tables:

- `posts`: Table to store the actual post's content.

- `authors`: Table to store the author's names. Each post belongs to one author and an author can have many posts.

- `categories`: Table to store the category names. Each post can belong to multiple categories and each category can have multiple posts.

- `posts_categories`: Table to store the relationship between `posts` and `categories`.

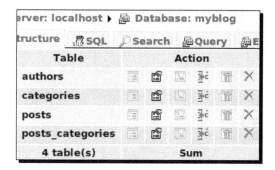

Time for action – populate the database tables

Populate all the tables with some dummy data. Make sure that you maintain the proper relationships in all the tables by inserting correct foreign keys in their respective fields.

```
INSERT INTO `posts` (`id`, `title`, `content`, `author_id`, `publish_
date`) VALUES
(1, 'Electronics For You', 'EFY- Electronics For You is a magazine for
people with a passion for Electronics and Technology. Since the first
issue in 1969, EFY has delivered the best in Product Reviews, Hardware
and Software comparisons, Technical News, Analysis, Electronics news,
about Products, Components, Computer Hardware,Power Supply, Industry
```

Automation, Circuit Designing provided by electronicsforu.com.', 2,
'2010-08-02 10:29:28'),
(2, 'What is PHP?', 'PHP Hypertext Preprocessor (the name is a
recursive acronym) is a widely used, general-purpose scripting
language that was originally designed for web development to produce
dynamic web pages.', 3, '2010-03-09 10:31:01'),
(3, 'Nintendo', 'Games that are easy to play and fun for anyone.
Nintendo are one of them major players in gaming world. They also
develop computer games these days.', 4, '2010-01-05 10:39:21'),
(4, 'Sony PlayStation - Full of life', 'Sony Playstation is one of
the leading gaming console of modern times. They are fun to play and
people of all age groups enjoy it.', 1, '2010-08-17 10:48:23'),
(5, 'Namespaces in PHP 5.3', 'One of the most significant and welcome
features added in PHP 5.3 was that of namespaces. While this has been
around in other programming languages, namespaces have finally found
their place starting with PHP 5.3.', 2, '2010-04-19 10:50:11'),
(6, 'Leadership Skills', 'Leadership skill is the key to success in
any field, be it software industry, automobile industry or any other
business.', 2, '2009-02-09 10:55:32'),
(7, 'Ruby on Rails', 'RoR is a rapid web application development
framework. It was one of the first framework for developing web
applications.', 4, '2010-08-13 13:44:32'),
(8, 'Sphinx search engine', 'Sphinx was created by Andrew Aksyonoff
and it can be used along with any programming language.', 1, '2009-04-
13 13:46:11');

INSERT INTO `authors` (`id`, `name`) VALUES
(1, 'Amit Badkas'),
(2, 'Aditya Mooley'),
(3, 'Rita Chouhan'),
(4, 'Dr.Tarique Sani');

INSERT INTO `categories` (`id`, `name`) VALUES
(1, 'Programming'),
(2, 'Games'),
(3, 'Electronics'),
(4, 'PHP'),
(5, 'Search'),
(6, 'Misc');

INSERT INTO `posts_categories` (`post_id`, `category_id`) VALUES
(1, 1),
(1, 2),

```
(1, 3),
(2, 1),
(2, 4),
(3, 2),
(3, 3),
(4, 2),
(4, 3),
(5, 1),
(5, 4),
(6, 6),
(7, 1),
(8, 1),
(8, 5);
```

What just happened?

We populated the database tables with some data. Later on we will index this data and search it using Sphinx.

In the real world this would be an application with some web frontend to manage the blog posts. Here we won't be looking into how to build that frontend as we are just focusing on the search part for now.

Time for action – creating the Sphinx configuration file

1. Create the file `/usr/local/sphinx/etc/sphinx-blog.conf` with the following content:

```
source blog
{
  type           = mysql

  sql_host       = localhost
  sql_user       = root
  sql_pass       =
  sql_db         = myblog

  sql_query       = SELECT id, title, content FROM posts

  sql_query_info   = SELECT id, title FROM posts WHERE ID=$id
}


index posts
```

```
{
  source           = blog
  path             = /usr/local/sphinx/var/data/blog
  docinfo          = extern
  charset_type     = sbcs
}


indexer
{
  mem_limit        = 32M
}
```

2. Run the following command to create the index:

```
$ /usr/local/sphinx/bin/indexer --config /usr/local/sphinx/etc/
sphinx-blog.conf --all
```

```
using config file '/usr/local/sphinx/etc/sphinx-blog.conf'...
indexing index 'posts'...
collected 8 docs, 0.0 MB
sorted 0.0 Mhits, 100.0% done
total 8 docs, 1543 bytes
total 0.007 sec, 195688 bytes/sec, 1014.58 docs/sec
total 1 reads, 0.000 sec, 1.9 kb/call avg, 0.0 msec/call avg
total 5 writes, 0.000 sec, 1.0 kb/call avg, 0.0 msec/call avg
```

3. Now test the index by searching from the command line search utility:

```
$ /usr/local/sphinx/bin/search --config /usr/local/sphinx/etc/
sphinx-blog.conf php
```

```
using config file '/usr/local/sphinx/etc/sphinx-blog.conf'...
index 'posts': query 'php ': returned 2 matches of 2 total in 0.000 sec

displaying matches:
1. document=2, weight=2
        id=2
        title=What is PHP?
2. document=5, weight=2
        id=5
        title=Namespaces in PHP 5.3

words:
1. 'php': 2 documents, 5 hits
```

What just happened?

We created a configuration file `/usr/local/sphinx/etc/sphinx-blog.conf`, which is later used by Sphinx to create an index.

The first block in the configuration file defines the data source named `blog` which is of type `mysql`. We provided values for the options to connect to the database and a query (`sql_query`) which fetches all the records from the database for indexing. The last option in the configuration file is `sql_query_info`, which is used to display additional information related to the searched documents. Because of this we see the `id` and `title` in the search results.

```
displaying matches:
1. document=2, weight=2
        id=2
        title=What is PHP?
```

The next block in the configuration file defines index. The index will be saved at `/usr/local/sphinx/var/data/blog` on the file system. To create the actual index we used the `indexer` program. `indexer` takes the path of the config file as the argument.

 If the config file path is not mentioned then it tries to search for it at the default location which is `/usr/local/sphinx/etc/sphinx.conf`.

Another argument we passed was `--all` which says that all indexes defined in the configuration file should be indexed. In our case there was just one index and we had named it `posts`.

There are a number of arguments that can be passed to the indexer. To view a list of all the arguments issue the following command:

```
$ /usr/local/sphinx/bin/indexer
```

```
Usage: indexer [OPTIONS] [indexname1 [indexname2 [...]]]

Options are:
--config <file>        read configuration from specified file
                       (default is sphinx.conf)
--all                  reindex all configured indexes
--quiet                be quiet, only print errors
--noprogress           do not display progress
                       (automatically on if output is not to a tty)
--rotate               send SIGHUP to searchd when indexing is over
                       to rotate updated indexes automatically
--buildstops <output.txt> <N>
                       build top N stopwords and write them to given file
--buildfreqs           store words frequencies to output.txt
                       (used with --buildstops only)
--merge <dst-index> <src-index>
                       merge 'src-index' into 'dst-index'
                       'dst-index' will receive merge result
                       'src-index' will not be modified
--merge-dst-range <attr> <min> <max>
                       filter 'dst-index' on merge, keep only those documents
                       where 'attr' is between 'min' and 'max' (inclusive)
--merge-killlists                       merge src and dst killlists instead of
Examples:
indexer --quiet myidx1  reindex 'myidx1' defined in 'sphinx.conf'
indexer --all           reindex all_indexes defined in 'sphinx.conf'
```

The last thing we did was perform a search for the term "php", which returned two documents. This concluded that our index is working fine.

The search utility used to perform the search is one of the helper tools available to quickly test the index from the command line without writing the code to connect to the searchd server and process its response.

search is not intended to be used in a client application. You should use searchd and the bundle client APIs to perform a search from within your application. We will be taking a look at how to use searchd and a client API to perform search in *Chapter 4, Searching*.

Similar to the indexer program, search also takes a number of arguments. Since we were not using the default configuration file, we passed the path of configuration file as an argument to the search command. The search term, that is "php", should always be last in the list of arguments.

```
$ /usr/local/sphinx/bin/search
```

```
Usage: search [OPTIONS] <word1 [word2 [word3 [...]]]>

Options are:
-c, --config <file>      use given config file instead of defaults
-i, --index <index>      search given index only (default: all indexes)
-a, --any                match any query word (default: match all words)
-b, --boolean            match in boolean mode
-p, --phrase             match exact phrase
-e, --extended           match in extended mode
-f, --filter <attr> <v>  only match if attribute attr value is v
-s, --sortby <CLAUSE>    sort matches by 'CLAUSE' in sort_extended mode
-S, --sortexpr <EXPR>    sort matches by 'EXPR' DESC in sort_expr mode
-o, --offset <offset>    print matches starting from this offset (default: 0)
-l, --limit <count>      print this many matches (default: 20)
-q, --noinfo             don't print document info from SQL database
-g, --group <attr>       group by attribute named attr
-gs,--groupsort <expr>   sort groups by <expr>
--sort=date              sort by date, descending
--rsort=date             sort by date, ascending
--sort=ts                sort by time segments
--stdin                  read query from stdin

This program (CLI search) is for testing and debugging purposes only;
it is NOT intended for production use.
```

The indexing workflow

Indexing works in the same fashion with all the SQL drivers. When `indexer` is run, a database connection is established using the credentials provided in the configuration file. After that, the main query, the `sql_query` is fired to fetch the data to be indexed. Once this is done the connection to the database is closed and the `indexer` does the sorting phase.

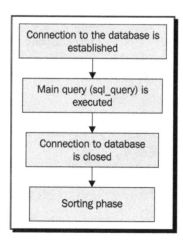

Adding attributes to the index

The index we created for the blog posts is all good and fine, but it only works for full-text searching. What if we want to filter the results by author or date? That can't be done with the index that we created earlier. To solve this problem, Sphinx offers special fields in the index called **attributes**.

Let's add attributes to our index to hold the author_id and publish_date.

Time for action – adding attributes to the index

1. Modify the file /usr/local/sphinx/etc/sphinx-blog.conf to add the code as highlighted next:

```
source blog
{
  type           = mysql

  sql_host       = localhost
  sql_user       = root
  sql_pass       =
  sql_db         = myblog

  sql_query          = \
    SELECT id, title, content, UNIX_TIMESTAMP(publish_date) \
    AS publish_date, author_id FROM posts

  sql_attr_uint            = author_id
  sql_attr_timestamp       = publish_date

  sql_query_info     = SELECT id, title FROM posts WHERE ID=$id
}


index posts
{
  source         = blog
  path           = /usr/local/sphinx/var/data/blog
  docinfo        = extern
  charset_type   = sbcs
}
```

```
indexer
{
  mem_limit        = 32M
}
```

 Backslashes (\) used for `sql_query` are just for clarity. The complete query can be written in one single line.

2. Run the `indexer` again to re-index the data:

   ```
   $ /usr/local/sphinx/bin/indexer --config /usr/local/sphinx/etc/
   sphinx-blog.conf --all
   ```

   ```
   using config file '/usr/local/sphinx/etc/sphinx-blog.conf'...
   indexing index 'posts'...
   collected 8 docs, 0.0 MB
   sorted 0.0 Mhits, 100.0% done
   total 8 docs, 1543 bytes
   total 0.014 sec, 105728 bytes/sec, 548.17 docs/sec
   total 2 reads, 0.000 sec, 1.0 kb/call avg, 0.0 msec/call avg
   total 7 writes, 0.000 sec, 0.7 kb/call avg, 0.0 msec/call avg
   ```

3. Search for all posts containing the term *php,* written by *Aditya Mooley* (`author_id = 2`):

   ```
   $ /usr/local/sphinx/bin/ search --config /usr/local/sphinx/etc/
   sphinx-blog.conf -f author_id 2 php
   ```

   ```
   using config file '/usr/local/sphinx/etc/sphinx-blog.conf'...
   index 'posts': query 'php ': returned 1 matches of 1 total in 0.000 sec

   displaying matches:
   1. document=5, weight=2, publish_date=Mon Apr 19 10:50:11 2010, author_id=2
           id=5
           title=Namespaces in PHP 5.3

   words:
   1. 'php': 2 documents, 5 hits
   ```

What just happened?

We modified the `sphinx-blog.conf` file, and changed the `sql_query` to fetch the `author_id` and `publish_date` along with other fields. We also added two new options; `sql_attr_unit` and `sql_attr_timestamp` to specify the two attributes. `author_id` is an unsigned integer, while `publish_date` is TIMESTAMP.

After that we re-indexed using the `indexer` command and this overwrote the previously created index file at `/usr/local/sphinx/var/data/blog`.

Now to filter our results by `author_id`, we specified the **–f** option to the search command that stands for filter. We filtered the results so that only those documents whose `author_id` attribute is **2** are returned.

 Filtering on timestamp attributes will be covered in *Chapter 4, Searching,* as that cannot be done using command line search utility.

Similarly if you want to filter the search results so that all documents, which contain the term "programming" but written by *Amit Badkas* (`author_id 1`) are returned—issue the following command:

```
$ /usr/local/sphinx/bin/search --config /usr/local/sphinx/etc/sphinx-
blog.conf -f author_id 1 programming
```

```
displaying matches:
1. document=8, weight=1, publish_date=Mon Apr 13 13:46:11 2009, author_id=1
        id=8
        title=Sphinx search engine

words:
1. 'programming': 2 documents, 2 hits
```

Adding an MVA to the index

We have already discussed filtering our results by authors. It was straight-forward since each post has only one author. However, what if we want to filter our results by categories? Remember, each post can be in one or more categories and we can only assign one value to an attribute. MVA comes to our rescue in these scenarios. As discussed earlier, an MVA can hold multiple values and we can filter our posts based on any of the categories they belong to.

Time for action – Adding an MVA to the index

1. Once again modify the `sphinx-blog.conf` file to add/modify the options as highlighted next:

```
source blog
{
  type           = mysql

  sql_host       = localhost
  sql_user       = root
  sql_pass       =
  sql_db         = myblog

  sql_query      = \
    SELECT id, title, content, UNIX_TIMESTAMP(publish_date) \
    AS publish_date, author_id FROM posts

  sql_attr_uint        = author_id
  sql_attr_multi       = uint category_id from query; \
        SELECT post_id, category_id FROM posts_categories
  sql_attr_timestamp   = publish_date

  sql_query_info       = SELECT id, title FROM posts WHERE ID=$id
}


index posts
{
  source         = blog
  path           = /usr/local/sphinx/var/data/blog
  docinfo        = extern
  charset_type   = sbcs
}


indexer
{
  mem_limit      = 32M
}
```

2. Run the `indexer` again to re-index the data:

```
$ /usr/local/sphinx/bin/indexer --config /usr/local/sphinx/etc/
sphinx-blog.conf --all
```

3. Search for all posts containing the term "language" and having the category "Search" (`category_id = 5`):

```
$ /usr/local/sphinx/bin/ search --config /usr/local/sphinx/etc/
sphinx-blog.conf -f category_id 5 language
```

```
using config file '/usr/local/sphinx/etc/sphinx-blog.conf'...
index 'posts': query 'language ': returned 1 matches of 1 total in 0.000
sec

displaying matches:
1. document=8, weight=1, publish_date=Mon Apr 13 13:46:11 2009, author_id
=1, category_id=(1,5)
        id=8
        title=Sphinx search engine

words:
1. 'language': 2 documents, 2 hits
```

What just happened?

We added a new option in source configuration called as `sql_attr_multi`. This option is used to declare the Multi valued attribute (MVA). This attribute only applies to SQL source types.

`sql_attr_multi` allows us to attach more than one value to an attribute. The format in which this option is declared is as follows:

```
sql_attr_multi = ATTR-TYPE ATTR-NAME 'from' SOURCE-TYPE [;QUERY]
[;RANGE-QUERY]
```

The option's parameters are as follows:

- ♦ ATTR-TYPE: Is `uint` or `timestamp`
- ♦ SOURCE-TYPE: Is 'field', 'query', or 'ranged-query'
- ♦ QUERY: Is an SQL query executed to fetch all `docid`, `attribute` value pairs
- ♦ RANGE-QUERY: Is SQL query used to fetch min and max ID values, similar to `sql_query_range`, which we will see later on

We declared `sql_attr_multi` as:

```
sql_attr_multi    = uint category_id from query; \
        SELECT post_id, category_id FROM posts_categories
```

This means that `category_id` is a `uint` attribute and will hold multiple values as returned by the query. The query that follows will get all the categories associated with the current post, such as the current document ID.

Let's search for all posts with any of the words from the string "web games php" having category "Programming" (`category_id` 1) and written by *Rita Chouhan* (`author_id` 3).

```
$ /usr/local/sphinx/bin/ search --config /usr/local/sphinx/etc/sphinx-
blog.conf -a -f category_id 1 -f author_id 3 web games php
```

```
using config file '/usr/local/sphinx/etc/sphinx-blog.conf'...
index 'posts': query 'web games php ': returned 1 matches of 1 total in 0
.000 sec

displaying matches:
1. document=2, weight=3, publish_date=Tue Mar  9 10:31:01 2010, author_id
=3, category_id=(1,4)
        id=2
        title=What is PHP?

words:
1. 'web': 2 documents, 4 hits
2. 'games': 1 documents, 2 hits
3. 'php': 2 documents, 5 hits
```

The previous search query returned the document ID 2 as the result. In the search query we used filters on two fields: `author_id` and `category_id`, and also used an option **–a** that specifically searched for any word from the given phrase.

The search result also shows us the number of documents Sphinx found for each word and the number of times (hits) each word appeared in those documents.

Filtering without searching for a specific phrase

At times we may want to only filter the results without performing a full-text search. For example: Find all posts with category PHP having any title or content, and written by any author. In such a case we don't have a specific search term, but we only want to filter by the `category_id` attribute. To achieve this we can issue a search command, as demonstrated in the following screenshot, without passing any search term:

```
$ /usr/local/sphinx/bin/ search --config /usr/local/sphinx/etc/sphinx-
blog.conf -f category_id 4
```

```
using config file '/usr/local/sphinx/etc/sphinx-blog.conf'...
index 'posts': query '': returned 2 matches of 2 total in 0.000 sec

displaying matches:
1. document=2, weight=1, publish_date=Tue Mar  9 10:31:01 2010, author_id
        id=2
        title=What is PHP?
2. document=5, weight=1, publish_date=Mon Apr 19 10:50:11 2010, author_id
        id=5
        title=Namespaces in PHP 5.3

words:
```

As we wanted to search for all posts having category PHP, we didn't pass the search term and just filtered the results by category_id. This gave us two documents with category_id = 4.

xmlpipe data source

xmlpipe data source enables users to implement their own data source drivers. At times we cannot use an SQL data source because the data might be coming from sources such as text files, mailboxes, RSS feeds, and so on. In such cases we can implement a custom driver using xmlpipe data source.

 xmlpipe data source is limited to two fixed fields and two fixed attributes, and above all, it is deprecated in favor of the xmlpipe2 data source explained in the next section.

We won't be going into the nitty-gritty of xmlpipe data source, instead, we will see how xmlpipe2 data source works in greater detail.

xmlpipe2 data source

xmlpipe2 is preferred over the older xmlpipe data source. It lets you pass arbitrary full-text and attribute data to Sphinx in a custom XML format. When the data source is configured to use xmlpipe2, indexer executes the given command and opens a pipe to its **stdout**. A well formed XML stream is then expected as the output of the command.

The XML schema (set of fields and attributes) can be defined either in the configuration file or the XML stream itself.

Indexing with schema defined in XML stream

Let's see how the xmlpipe2 data source is configured and what XML the `indexer` expects at the **stdout** of the given command.

 We are going to continue with the same blog example as used in the *SQL data sources* section earlier in this chapter.

Firstly, let's see how to index the `posts` table without any attributes.

Time for action – creating index (without attributes)

1. Create a new Sphinx configuration file at `/usr/local/sphinx/etc/sphinx-blog-xmlpipe2.conf` with the following options:

```
source blog
{
  type            = xmlpipe2
  xmlpipe_command = /usr/bin/php /home/abbas/sphinx/makeindex.php
}


index posts
{
  source          = blog
  path            = /usr/local/sphinx/var/data/blog-xmlpipe2
  docinfo         = extern
  charset_type    = utf-8
}


indexer
{
  mem_limit       = 32M
}
```

2. Create the PHP script `/home/abbas/sphinx/makeindex.php` (this script can be anywhere on your machine).

```php
<?php
// Database connection credentials
$dsn  ='mysql:dbname=myblog;host=localhost';
$user = 'root';
$pass = '';

// Instantiate the PDO (PHP 5 specific) class
```

```
try {
    $dbh = new PDO($dsn, $user, $pass);
} catch (PDOException $e){
    echo'Connection failed: '.$e->getMessage();
}

// We will use PHP's inbuilt XMLWriter to create the xml structure
$xmlwriter = new XMLWriter();
$xmlwriter->openMemory();
$xmlwriter->setIndent(true);
$xmlwriter->startDocument('1.0', 'UTF-8');
// Start the parent docset element
$xmlwriter->startElement('sphinx:docset');

// Start the element for schema definition
$xmlwriter->startElement('sphinx:schema');

// Start the element for title field
$xmlwriter->startElement('sphinx:field');
$xmlwriter->writeAttribute("name", "title");
$xmlwriter->endElement(); //end field

// Start the element for content field
$xmlwriter->startElement('sphinx:field');
$xmlwriter->writeAttribute("name", "content");
$xmlwriter->endElement(); //end field

$xmlwriter->endElement(); //end schema

// Query to get all posts from the database
$sql = "SELECT id, title, content FROM posts";

// Run a loop and put the post data in XML
foreach ($dbh->query($sql) as $post) {
    // Start the element for holding the actual document (post)
    $xmlwriter->startElement('sphinx:document');
    // Add the id attribute
    $xmlwriter->writeAttribute("id", $post['id']);

    // Set value for the title field
    $xmlwriter->startElement('title');
    $xmlwriter->text($post['title']);
    $xmlwriter->endElement();//end title
```

```
        // Set value for the content field
        $xmlwriter->startElement('content');
        $xmlwriter->text($post['content']);
        $xmlwriter->endElement();// end content

        $xmlwriter->endElement();// end document
    }

    $xmlwriter->endElement();// end docset

    // Output the xml
    print $xmlwriter->flush();
    ?>
```

3. Run the `indexer` to create the index:

```
$ /usr/local/sphinx/bin/indexer --config /usr/local/sphinx/etc/
sphinx-blog-xmlpipe2.conf --all
```

```
using config file '/usr/local/sphinx/etc/sphinx-blog-xmlpipe2.conf'...
indexing index 'posts'...
collected 8 docs, 0.0 MB
sorted 0.0 Mhits, 100.0% done
total 8 docs, 1543 bytes
total 0.009 sec, 158305 bytes/sec, 820.76 docs/sec
total 1 reads, 0.000 sec, 1.9 kb/call avg, 0.0 msec/call avg
total 5 writes, 0.000 sec, 1.0 kb/call avg, 0.0 msec/call avg
```

4. Test the index by searching for "programming":

```
$ /usr/local/sphinx/bin/search --config /usr/local/sphinx/etc/
xmlpipe2.conf programming
```

```
using config file '/usr/local/sphinx/etc/sphinx-blog-xmlpipe2.conf'...
index 'posts': query 'programming ': returned 2 matches of 2 total in 0.00

displaying matches:
1. document=5, weight=1
2. document=8, weight=1

words:
1. 'programming': 2 documents, 2 hits
```

What just happened?

The xmlpipe2 data source needs an option `xmlpipe_command`, which should be the command to be executed, that streams the XML on its `stdout`. In our case, we are using the PHP script `/home/abbas/sphinx/makeindex.php` to create the well-formed XML. This script is executed using the PHP CLI located at `/usr/bin/php`.

 You may put the PHP script anywhere on your file system. Just make sure to use the correct path in your configuration file.

 To determine the path to PHP CLI, you can issue the following command:
`$ which php`

No other option is required in the data source configuration if we are specifying the schema in the XML itself.

Next we created the PHP script which outputs the well-formed XML. In the script we first connected to the database and retrieved all posts using the PHP 5 native PDO driver. We created the XML structure with the help of PHP's XMLWriter class.

 An explanation of how the PHP code works is beyond the scope of this book. Please refer to the PHP Manual (`http://www.php.net/manual/`) for more details.

The output (text truncated for brevity) of our PHP script looks something like this:

```xml
<?xml version="1.0" encoding="UTF-8"?>
<sphinx:docset>
 <sphinx:schema>
  <sphinx:field name="title"/>
  <sphinx:field name="content"/>
 </sphinx:schema>
 <sphinx:document id="1">
  <title>Electronics For You</title>
  <content>EFY- Electronics For You is a magazine for people with a
passion for Electronics and Technology...</content>
 </sphinx:document>
 <sphinx:document id="2">
  <title>What is PHP?</title>
  <content>PHP Hypertext Preprocessor...</content>
 </sphinx:document>
```

```
<!-- ... remaining documents here ... -->

</sphinx:docset>
```

The XML structure is pretty much self explanatory. We specified the schema (fields and attributes to be added to the index) at the top using the `<sphinx:schema>` element. It is compulsory to declare the schema before any document is parsed. Arbitrary fields and attributes are allowed, and they can occur in the stream in arbitrary order within each document.

 `<sphinx:schema>` is only allowed to occur as the very first sub-element in `<sphinx:docset>`. However, it is optional and can be omitted if settings are defined in configuration file.

If the schema is already declared in the configuration file then there's no need to declare it in the XML structure. In-stream schema definition takes precedence and if there is no in-stream definition, then settings from the configuration file will be used.

Any unknown XML tags, such as the tags, which were neither declared as fields nor as attributes, will be ignored and won't make it to the index.

The following are the XML elements (tags) used in the previous code snippet. They are recognized by xmlpipe2:

- `sphinx:docset`: Mandatory top-level element. It contains the document set for xmlpipe2.

- `sphinx:schema`: Optional, must occur as the first child of docset or never occur at all. It contains field and attribute declarations, and defines the document schema. It overrides the settings from the configuration file.

- `sphinx:field`: Optional, child of sphinx:schema. It declares a full-text field and its only recognized attribute is **name**, which specifies the element name that should be treated as a full-text field in the subsequent documents.

- `sphinx:document`: This is a mandatory element which holds the actual data to be indexed. It must be the child of the `sphinx:docset` element. This element can contain arbitrary sub-elements with field and attribute values to be indexed (as declared either in `sphinx:schema` or configuration file). The compulsory known attribute of this element is **id**. It must contain the unique integer document ID.

Once the index stands created, we perform a search for the usual way using the command line utility.

 We don't get extra information like `title` in search results output since that was SQL data-source specific. `sql_query_info` was used to fetch that extra information and that cannot be used with xmlpipe2 data source.

Now, let's see how to define attributes in `sphinx:schema` so that the same goes in our index.

Time for action – add attributes to schema

1. Modify `/home/abbas/sphinx/makeindex.php` file and make the changes as highlighted next:

```php
<?php
// Database connection credentials
$dsn  ='mysql:dbname=myblog;host=localhost';
$user = 'root';
$pass = '';

// Instantiate the PDO (PHP 5 specific) class
try {
    $dbh = new PDO($dsn, $user, $pass);
} catch (PDOException $e){
    echo'Connection failed: '.$e->getMessage();
}

// We will use PHP's inbuilt XMLWriter to create the xml structure
$xmlwriter = new XMLWriter();
$xmlwriter->openMemory();
$xmlwriter->setIndent(true);
$xmlwriter->startDocument('1.0', 'UTF-8');
// Start the parent docset element
$xmlwriter->startElement('sphinx:docset');

// Start the element for schema definition
$xmlwriter->startElement('sphinx:schema');

// Start the element for title field
$xmlwriter->startElement('sphinx:field');
$xmlwriter->writeAttribute("name", "title");
$xmlwriter->endElement(); //end field
```

```
// Start the element for content field
$xmlwriter->startElement('sphinx:field');
$xmlwriter->writeAttribute("name", "content");
$xmlwriter->endElement(); //end field

// Start the element for author_id attribute
$xmlwriter->startElement('sphinx:attr');
$xmlwriter->writeAttribute("name", "author_id");
$xmlwriter->writeAttribute("type", "int");
$xmlwriter->endElement(); //end attribute

// Start the element for timestamp attribute
$xmlwriter->startElement('sphinx:attr');
$xmlwriter->writeAttribute("name", "publish_date");
$xmlwriter->writeAttribute("type", "timestamp");
$xmlwriter->endElement(); //end attribute

// Start the element for multi valued category_id attribute
$xmlwriter->startElement('sphinx:attr');
$xmlwriter->writeAttribute("name", "category_id");
$xmlwriter->writeAttribute("type", "multi");
$xmlwriter->endElement(); //end attribute


$xmlwriter->endElement(); //end schema

// Query to get all posts from the database
$sql = "SELECT id, title, content, author_id, UNIX_
TIMESTAMP(publish_date) AS publish_date FROM posts";
$posts = $dbh->query($sql);
// Run a loop and put the post data in XML
foreach ($posts as $post) {
    // Start the element for holding the actual document (post)
    $xmlwriter->startElement('sphinx:document');
    // Add the id attribute
    $xmlwriter->writeAttribute("id", $post['id']);

    // Set value for the title field
    $xmlwriter->startElement('title');
    $xmlwriter->text($post['title']);
    $xmlwriter->endElement();//end title
```

```php
        // Set value for the content field
        $xmlwriter->startElement('content');
        $xmlwriter->text($post['content']);
        $xmlwriter->endElement();// end content

        // Set value for the author_id attribute
        $xmlwriter->startElement('author_id');
        $xmlwriter->text($post['author_id']);
        $xmlwriter->endElement();// end attribute

        // Set value for the publish_date attribute
        $xmlwriter->startElement('publish_date');
        $xmlwriter->text($post['publish_date']);
        $xmlwriter->endElement();// end attribute

        // Find all categories associated with this post
        $catsql = "SELECT category_id FROM posts_categories "
              . " WHERE post_id = {$post['id']}";
        $categories = array();
        foreach ($dbh->query($catsql) as $category) {
            $categories[] = $category['category_id'];
        }
        // Set value for the category_id attribute
        // Multiple category ids should be comma separated
        $xmlwriter->startElement('category_id');
        $xmlwriter->text(implode(',', $categories));
        $xmlwriter->endElement();// end attribute

        $xmlwriter->endElement();// end document
    }

    $xmlwriter->endElement();// end docset

    // Output the xml
    print $xmlwriter->flush();
    ?>
```

2. Run the `indexer` to re-create the index:

```
$ /usr/local/sphinx/bin/indexer --config /usr/local/sphinx/etc/
sphinx-blog-xmlpipe2.conf --all
```

```
using config file '/usr/local/sphinx/etc/sphinx-blog-xmlpipe2.conf'...
indexing index 'posts'...
collected 8 docs, 0.0 MB
collected 15 attr values
sorted 0.0 Mvalues, 100.0% done
sorted 0.0 Mhits, 100.0% done
total 8 docs, 1543 bytes
total 0.032 sec, 47957 bytes/sec, 248.64 docs/sec
total 3 reads, 0.000 sec, 0.7 kb/call avg, 0.0 msec/call avg
total 9 writes, 0.000 sec, 0.6 kb/call avg, 0.0 msec/call avg
```

3. Search for posts containing the word "programming" and having category "PHP"
(`category_id` 4).

```
$ /usr/local/sphinx/bin/search --config /usr/local/sphinx/etc/
sphinx-blog-xmlpipe2.conf -f category_id 4 programming
```

```
using config file '../etc/sphinx-blog-xmlpipe2.conf'...
index 'posts': query 'programming ': returned 1 matches of 1 total in 0.0
00 sec

displaying matches:
1. document=5, weight=1, author_id=2, publish_date=Mon Apr 19 10:50:11 20
10, category_id=(1,4)

words:
1. 'programming': 2 documents, 2 hits
```

What just happened?

We modified our PHP script, which streams the XML, to include the attribute definition as
well as attribute values. We included the following attributes:

- `author_id`: Uint
- `publish_date`: Timestamp
- `category_id`: Multi valued attribute (MVA). We provided multiple category IDs as
  a comma separated value.

The new XML stream looks like this:

```xml
<?xml version="1.0" encoding="UTF-8"?>
<sphinx:docset>
 <sphinx:schema>
  <sphinx:field name="title"/>
  <sphinx:field name="content"/>
  <sphinx:attr name="author_id" type="int"/>
  <sphinx:attr name="publish_date" type="timestamp"/>
```

```
  <sphinx:attr name="category_id" type="multi"/>
 </sphinx:schema>
 <sphinx:document id="1">
  <title>Electronics For You</title>
  <content>EFY- Electronics For You is a magazine for people with a
 passion for Electronics and Technology…</content>
  <author_id>2</author_id>
  <publish_date>1280725168</publish_date>
  <category_id>1,2,3</category_id>
 </sphinx:document>
 <sphinx:document id="2">
  <title>What is PHP?</title>
  <content>PHP Hypertext Preprocessor...</content>
  <author_id>3</author_id>
  <publish_date>1268110861</publish_date>
  <category_id>1,4</category_id>
 </sphinx:document>

<!-- ... remaining documents here ... -->

</sphinx:docset>
```

The new XML element used here is **sphinx:attr** which is an optional element, and if present, must be a child of sphinx:schema. This element is used to declare an attribute of the document in the index. Known attributes of this sphinx:attr element are:

- name: Specifies the name that should be treated as an attribute in the subsequent documents.

- type: Specifies the attribute type. The possible values of this attribute are int, timestamp, str2ordinal, bool, float, and multi.

- bits: Specifies the bit size for int attribute and value values are 1 to 32.

- default: Specifies the default value that should be used if the attribute's respective element is not present in the document.

Don't confuse yourself with an attribute of XML element and an attribute in the index.

For example: <sphinx:attr name="author_id">

Here the XML element attribute is name, while the attribute that goes into the index is author_id.

After making the necessary changes in `makeindex.php`, we re-created the index. There was no need to make any changes in the configuration file as the schema was defined in the XML itself instead of configuration file.

With attributes in place, we performed a search for posts containing the word "programming" and having category as "PHP", or in other words, filtered the results by `category_id`.

Indexing with schema defined in configuration file

Now let's see how to define the schema (fields and attributes) in the Sphinx configuration file, instead of defining it in the XML stream. This is very similar to what we did when we used SQL data sources and defined the attributes in the source block of the configuration file.

Time for action – create index with schema defined in configuration file

1. Modify `/usr/local/sphinx/etc/sphinx-blog-xmlpipe2.conf` and include the fields and attributes definition in the `source` block:

```
source blog
{
  type           = xmlpipe2
  xmlpipe_command = /usr/bin/php /home/abbas/sphinx/makeindex.php
  xmlpipe_field    = title
  xmlpipe_field    = content
  xmlpipe_attr_uint = author_id
  xmlpipe_attr_timestamp = publish_date
  xmlpipe_attr_multi = category_id
}

index posts
{
  source           = blog
  path             = /usr/local/sphinx/var/data/blog-xmlpipe2
  docinfo          = extern
  charset_type     = utf-8
}

indexer
{
  mem_limit        = 32M
}
```

2. Modify the `makeindex.php` script and remove the **sphinx:schema** element along with all its sub-elements:

```php
<?php
// Database connection credentials
$dsn  ='mysql:dbname=myblog;host=localhost';
$user = 'root';
$pass = '';

// Instantiate the PDO (PHP 5 specific) class
try {
    $dbh = new PDO($dsn, $user, $pass);
} catch (PDOException $e){
    echo'Connection failed: '.$e->getMessage();
}

// We will use PHP's inbuilt XMLWriter to create the xml structure
$xmlwriter = new XMLWriter();
$xmlwriter->openMemory();
$xmlwriter->setIndent(true);
$xmlwriter->startDocument('1.0', 'UTF-8');
// Start the parent docset element
$xmlwriter->startElement('sphinx:docset');

// Query to get all posts from the database
$sql = "SELECT id, title, content, author_id, UNIX_
TIMESTAMP(publish_date) AS publish_date FROM posts";
$posts = $dbh->query($sql);
// Run a loop and put the post data in XML
foreach ($posts as $post) {
    // Start the element for holding the actual document (post)
    $xmlwriter->startElement('sphinx:document');
    // Add the id attribute
    $xmlwriter->writeAttribute("id", $post['id']);

    // Set value for the title field
    $xmlwriter->startElement('title');
    $xmlwriter->text($post['title']);
    $xmlwriter->endElement();//end title

    // Set value for the content field
    $xmlwriter->startElement('content');
    $xmlwriter->text($post['content']);
    $xmlwriter->endElement();// end content
```

```
    // Set value for the author_id attribute
    $xmlwriter->startElement('author_id');
    $xmlwriter->text($post['author_id']);
    $xmlwriter->endElement();// end attribute

    // Set value for the publish_date attribute
    $xmlwriter->startElement('publish_date');
    $xmlwriter->text($post['publish_date']);
    $xmlwriter->endElement();// end attribute

    // Find all categories associated with this post
    $catsql = "SELECT category_id FROM posts_categories WHERE
post_id = {$post['id']}";
    $categories = array();
    foreach ($dbh->query($catsql) as $category) {
        $categories[] = $category['category_id'];
    }
    // Set value for the category_id attribute
    // Multiple category ids should be comma separated
    $xmlwriter->startElement('category_id');
    $xmlwriter->text(implode(',', $categories));
    $xmlwriter->endElement();// end attribute

    $xmlwriter->endElement();// end document
}

$xmlwriter->endElement();// end docset

// Output the xml
print $xmlwriter->flush();
?>
```

3. Create the index using the indexer:

```
$ /usr/local/sphinx/bin/indexer --config /usr/local/sphinx/etc/
sphinx-blog-xmlpipe2.conf --all
```

What just happened?

We added the schema definition, and the declaration of fields and attributes that goes into index, in the configuration file itself.

To define a field we used the `xmlpipe_field` option and to define an attribute we used the `xmlpipe_attr_*` option. The following are some of the attribute options that can be used:

- `xmlpipe_attr_uint`: For unsigned integers. Syntax matches that for `sql_attr_uint`.

- `xmlpipe_attr_bool`: For Boolean attributes. Syntax matches that for `sql_attr_bool`.

- `xmlpipe_attr_timestamp`: For UNIX timestamp attributes. Syntax matches that for `sql_attr_timestamp`.

- `xmlpipe_attr_str2ordinal`: For string ordinal attributes. Syntax matches that of `sql_attr_str2ordinal`.

- `xmlpipe_attr_float`: For floating point attributes. Syntax matches that of `sql_attr_float`.

- `xmlpipe_attr_multi`: For Multi Valued Attributes (MVA).

We then removed the `<sphinx:schema>` element from the XML stream by modifying our `makeindex.php` script.

 If the schema is defined at both places, that is, in the configuration file as well as the XML stream then schema in XML stream takes precedence.

No other change was required in the XML stream.

Summary

In this chapter:

- ◆ We saw what indexes are and how they are used in Sphinx
- ◆ We learned about fields and the different kind of attributes that go into the index
- ◆ We took a look at how to create the Sphinx configuration file
- ◆ We learned about SQL data source and xmlpipe data source
- ◆ We learned how to use different kind of attributes so that we can filter our search results

In the next chapter we will see how to use the Sphinx API to search from within your application. We will use the same index used in this chapter and fire queries from our PHP application to get the results.

4
Searching

In the previous chapter we learned how to create indexes. Now let's see how to search those indexes from within your applications.

In this chapter we will learn how to use the Sphinx API to issue search queries from your PHP applications. We will examine different query syntaxes and learn about weighting, sorting, and grouping our search results.

We will be using the indexes created in *Chapter 3*, *Indexing* and write search queries to search those indexes.

Client API implementations for Sphinx

Sphinx comes with a number of native `searchd` client API implementations. At the time of writing this book, Sphinx came with PHP, Python, and Java implementations. Some third-party open source implementations for Perl, Ruby, and C++ are also available.

All APIs provide the same set of methods and they implement the same network protocol. As a result, they more or less all work in a similar fashion, they all work in a similar fashion.

 All examples in this chapter are for PHP implementation of the Sphinx API. However, you can just as easily use other programming languages.

Sphinx is used with PHP more widely than any other language.

Search using client API

Let's see how we can use native PHP implementation of Sphinx API to search. We will be using the index and configuration file created in *Chapter 3, Indexing*. We will add a configuration related to `searchd` and then create a PHP file to search the index using the Sphinx client API implementation for PHP.

Time for action – creating a basic search script

1. Add the `searchd` config section to `/usr/local/sphinx/etc/sphinx-blog.conf`:

```
source blog {
  # source options
}

index posts {
  # index options
}

indexer {
  # indexer options
}

# searchd options (used by search daemon)
searchd
{
  listen        = 9312
  log           = /usr/local/sphinx/var/log/searchd.log
  query_log     = /usr/local/sphinx/var/log/query.log
  max_children  = 30
  pid_file      = /usr/local/sphinx/var/log/searchd.pid
}
```

2. Start the `searchd` daemon (as root user):

```
$ sudo /usr/local/sphinx/bin/searchd -c /usr/local/sphinx/etc/
sphinx-blog.conf
```

```
Sphinx 0.9.9-release (r2117)
Copyright (c) 2001-2009, Andrew Aksyonoff

using config file '/usr/local/sphinx/etc/sphinx-blog.conf'...
listening on all interfaces, port=9312
```

3. Copy the `sphinxapi.php` file (the class with PHP implementation of Sphinx API) from the sphinx source directory to your working directory:

```
$ mkdir /path/to/your/webroot/sphinx

$ cd /path/to/your/webroot/sphinx

$ cp /path/to/sphinx-0.9.9/api/sphinxapi.php ./
```

4. Create a `simple_search.php` script that uses the PHP client API class to search the Sphinx-blog index, and execute it in the browser:

```php
<?php
require_once('sphinxapi.php');
// Instantiate the sphinx client
$client = new SphinxClient();
// Set search options
$client->SetServer('localhost', 9312);
$client->SetConnectTimeout(1);
$client->SetArrayResult(true);

// Query the index
$results = $client->Query('php');

// Output the matched results in raw format
print_r($results['matches']);
```

5. The output of the given code, as seen in a browser, will be similar to what's shown in the following screenshot:

```
Array
(
    [error] =>
    [warning] =>
    [status] => 0
    [fields] => Array
        (
            [0] => title
            [1] => content
        )

    [attrs] => Array
        (
            [publish_date] => 2
            [author_id] => 1
            [category_id] => 1073741825
        )

    [matches] => Array
        (
            [0] => Array
                (
                    [id] => 2
                    [weight] => 2
                    [attrs] => Array
                        (
                            [publish_date] => 1268110861
                            [author_id] => 3
                            [category_id] => Array
                                (
                                    [0] => 1
                                    [1] => 4
                                )

                        )

                )

            [1] => Array
                (
                    [id] => 5
                    [weight] => 2
                    [attrs] => Array
                        (
                            [publish_date] => 1271654411
                            [author_id] => 2
                            [category_id] => Array
                                (
                                    [0] => 1
                                    [1] => 4
                                )

                        )

                )

        )

    [total] => 2
    [total_found] => 2
    [time] => 0.001
    [words] => Array
        (
            [php] => Array
```

What just happened?

Firstly, we added the searchd configuration section to our sphinx-blog.conf file (created in *Chapter 3, Indexing*). The following options were added to searchd section:

- ◆ listen: This options specifies the IP address and port that searchd will listen on. It can also specify the Unix-domain socket path. This options was introduced in v0.9.9 and should be used instead of the port (deprecated) option. If the port part is omitted, then the default port used is 9312.

  Examples:

  - ❏ listen = localhost
  - ❏ listen = 9312
  - ❏ listen = localhost:9898
  - ❏ listen = 192.168.1.25:4000
  - ❏ listen = /var/run/sphinx.s

- ◆ log: Name of the file where all searchd runtime events will be logged. This is an optional setting and the default value is "searchd.log".

- ◆ query_log: Name of the file where all search queries will be logged. This is an optional setting and the default value is empty, that is, do not log queries.

- ◆ max_children: The maximum number of concurrent searches to run in parallel. This is an optional setting and the default value is 0 (unlimited).

- ◆ pid_file: Filename of the searchd process ID. This is a mandatory setting. The file is created on startup and it contains the head daemon process ID while the daemon is running. The pid_file becomes unlinked when the daemon is stopped.

Once we were done with adding searchd configuration options, we started the searchd daemon with root user. We passed the path of the configuration file as an argument to searchd. The default configuration file used is /usr/local/sphinx/etc/sphinx.conf.

After a successful startup, searchd listens on all network interfaces, including all the configured network cards on the server, at port 9312. If we want searchd to listen on a specific interface then we can specify the hostname or IP address in the value of the listen option:

```
listen = 192.168.1.25:9312
```

 The listen setting defined in the configuration file can be overridden in the command line while starting searchd by using the -l command line argument.

There are other (optional) arguments that can be passed to `searchd` as seen in the following screenshot:

```
Usage: searchd [OPTIONS]

Options are:
-h, --help              display this help message
-c, -config <file>      read configuration from specified file
                        (default is sphinx.conf)
--stop                  send SIGTERM to currently running searchd
--status                get ant print status variables
                        (PID is taken from pid_file specified in config file)
--iostats               log per-query io stats
--cpustats              log per-query cpu stats

Debugging options are:
--console               run in console mode (do not fork, do not log to files)
-p, --port <port>       listen on given port (overrides config setting)
-l, --listen <spec>     listen on given address, port or path (overrides
                        config settings)
-i, --index <index>     only serve one given index
--nodetach              do not detach into background
```

 searchd needs to be running all the time when we are using the client API. The first thing you should always check is whether `searchd` is running or not, and start it if it is not running.

We then created a PHP script to search the sphinx-blog index. To search the Sphinx index, we need to use the Sphinx client API. As we are working with a PHP script, we copied the PHP client implementation class, (`sphinxapi.php`) which comes along with Sphinx source, to our working directory so that we can include it in our script. However, you can keep this file anywhere on the file system as long as you can include it in your PHP script.

 Throughout this book we will be using `/path/to/webroot/sphinx` as the working directory and we will create all PHP scripts in that directory. We will refer to this directory simply as **webroot**.

We initialized the `SphinxClient` class and then used the following class methods to set up the Sphinx client API:

◆ `SphinxClient::SetServer($host, $port)`—This method sets the `searchd` hostname and port. All subsequent requests use these settings unless this method is called again with some different parameters. The default host is `localhost` and port is `9312`.

- ◆ SphinxClient::SetConnectTimeout($timeout)—This is the maximum time allowed to spend trying to connect to the server before giving up.
- ◆ SphinxClient::SetArrayResult($arrayresult)—This is a PHP client API-specific method. It specifies whether the matches should be returned as an array or a hash. The Default value is false, which means that matches will be returned in a PHP hash format, where document IDs will be the keys, and other information (attributes, weight) will be the values. If $arrayresult is true, then the matches will be returned in plain arrays with complete per-match information.

After that, the actual querying of index was pretty straightforward using the **SphinxClient::Query($query)** method. It returned an array with matched results, as well as other information such as error, fields in index, attributes in index, total records found, time taken for search, and so on. The actual results are in the **$results['matches']** variable.

We can run a loop on the results, and it is a straightforward job to get the actual document's content from the document ID and display it.

Matching modes

When a full-text search is performed on the Sphinx index, different matching modes can be used by Sphinx to find the results. The following matching modes are supported by Sphinx:

- ◆ SPH_MATCH_ALL—This is the default mode and it matches all query words, that is, only records that match all of the queried words will be returned.
- ◆ SPH_MATCH_ANY—This matches any of the query words.
- ◆ SPH_MATCH_PHRASE—This matches query as a phrase and requires a perfect match.
- ◆ SPH_MATCH_BOOLEAN—This matches query as a Boolean expression.
- ◆ SPH_MATCH_EXTENDED—This matches query as an expression in Sphinx internal query language.
- ◆ SPH_MATCH_EXTENDED2—This matches query using the second version of Extended matching mode. This supersedes SPH_MATCH_EXTENDED as of v0.9.9.
- ◆ SPH_MATCH_FULLSCAN—In this mode the query terms are ignored and no text-matching is done, but filters and grouping are still applied.

Time for action – searching with different matching modes

1. Create a PHP script `display_results.php` in your `webroot` with the following code:

```php
<?php
// Database connection credentials
$dsn  ='mysql:dbname=myblog;host=localhost';
$user = 'root';
$pass = '';

// Instantiate the PDO (PHP 5 specific) class
try {
    $dbh = new PDO($dsn, $user, $pass);
} catch (PDOException $e){
    echo'Connection failed: '.$e->getMessage();
}
// PDO statement to fetch the post data
$query = "SELECT p.*, a.name FROM posts AS p " .
        "LEFT JOIN authors AS a ON p.author_id = a.id " .
        "WHERE p.id = :post_id";
$post_stmt = $dbh->prepare($query);

// PDO statement to fetch the post's categories
$query = "SELECT c.name FROM posts_categories AS pc ".
        "LEFT JOIN categories AS c ON pc.category_id = c.id " .
        "WHERE pc.post_id = :post_id";
$cat_stmt = $dbh->prepare($query);

// Function to display the results in a nice format
function display_results($results, $message = null)
{
    global $post_stmt, $cat_stmt;
    if ($message) {
        print "<h3>$message</h3>";
    }
    if (!isset($results['matches'])) {
        print "No results found<hr />";
        return;
    }
    foreach ($results['matches'] as $result) {
        // Get the data for this document (post) from db
        $post_stmt->bindParam(':post_id',
            $result['id'],
            PDO::PARAM_INT);
```

```
$post_stmt->execute();
$post = $post_stmt->fetch(PDO::FETCH_ASSOC);

// Get the categories of this post
$cat_stmt->bindParam(':post_id',
    $result['id'],
    PDO::PARAM_INT);
$cat_stmt->execute();
$categories = $cat_stmt->fetchAll(PDO::FETCH_ASSOC);

// Output title, author and categories
print "Id: {$posmt['id']}<br />" .
    "Title: {$post['title']}<br />" .
    "Author: {$post['name']}";
$cats = array();
foreach ($categories as $category) {
    $cats[] = $category['name'];
}
if (count($cats)) {
    print "<br />Categories: " . implode(', ', $cats);
}
print "<hr />";
    }
}
```

2. Create a PHP script search_matching_modes.php in your webroot with the
    following code:

```
<?php
// Include the api class
Require('sphinxapi.php');
// Include the file which contains the function to display results
require_once('display_results.php');

$client = new SphinxClient();
// Set search options
$client->SetServer('localhost', 9312);
$client->SetConnectTimeout(1);
$client->SetArrayResult(true);

// SPH_MATCH_ALL mode will be used by default
// and we need not set it explicitly
display_results(
$client->Query('php'),
'"php" with SPH_MATCH_ALL');
```

```
display_results(
$client->Query('programming'),
'"programming" with SPH_MATCH_ALL');

display_results(
$client->Query('php programming'),
'"php programming" with SPH_MATCH_ALL');

// Set the mode to SPH_MATCH_ANY
$client->SetMatchMode(SPH_MATCH_ANY);

display_results(
$client->Query('php programming'),
'"php programming" with SPH_MATCH_ANY');

// Set the mode to SPH_MATCH_PHRASE
$client->SetMatchMode(SPH_MATCH_PHRASE);

display_results(
$client->Query('php programming'),
'"php programming" with SPH_MATCH_PHRASE');

display_results(
$client->Query('scripting language'),
'"scripting language" with SPH_MATCH_PHRASE');

// Set the mode to SPH_MATCH_FULLSCAN
$client->SetMatchMode(SPH_MATCH_FULLSCAN);

display_results(
$client->Query('php'),
'"php programming" with SPH_MATCH_FULLSCAN');
```

3. Execute `search_matching_modes.php` in a browser (`http://localhost/sphinx/search_matching_modes.php`).

What just happened?

The first thing we did was created a script, `display_results.php`, which connects to the database and gathers additional information on related posts. This script has a function, `display_results()` that outputs the Sphinx results returned in a nice format. The code is pretty much self explanatory.

Next, we created the PHP script that actually performs the search. We used the following matching modes and queried using different search terms:

◆ SPH_MATCH_ALL (Default mode which doesn't need to be explicitly set)

◆ SPH_MATCH_ANY

◆ SPH_MATCH_PHRASE

◆ SPH_MATCH_FULLSCAN

Let's see what the output of each query was and try to understand it:

```
display_results(
    $client->Query('php'),
    '"php" with SPH_MATCH_ALL');

display_results(
    $client->Query('programming'),
    '"programming" with SPH_MATCH_ALL');
```

The output for these two queries can be seen in the following screenshot:

"php" with SPH_MATCH_ALL

Id: 2
Title: What is PHP?
Author: Rita Chouhan
Categories: Programming, PHP

Id: 5
Title: Namespaces in PHP 5.3
Author: Aditya Mooley
Categories: Programming, PHP

"programming" with SPH_MATCH_ALL

Id: 5
Title: Namespaces in PHP 5.3
Author: Aditya Mooley
Categories: Programming, PHP

Id: 8
Title: Sphinx search engine
Author: Amit Badkas
Categories: Programming, Search

The first two queries returned all posts containing the words "php" and "programming" respectively. We got posts with id **2** and **5** for "php", and **5** and **8** for "programming".

The third query was for posts containing both words, that is "php programming", and it returned the following result:

```
"php programming" with SPH_MATCH_ALL

Id: 5
Title: Namespaces in PHP 5.3
Author: Aditya Mooley
Categories: Programming, PHP
```

This time we only got posts with id **5**, as this was the only post containing both the words of the phrase "php programming".

We used `SPH_MATCH_ANY` to search for any words of the search phrase:

```
// Set the mode to SPH_MATCH_ANY
$client->SetMatchMode(SPH_MATCH_ANY);

display_results(
    $client->Query('php programming'),
    '"php programming" with SPH_MATCH_ANY');
```

The function call returns the following output (results):

```
"php programming" with SPH_MATCH_ANY

Id: 5
Title: Namespaces in PHP 5.3
Author: Aditya Mooley
Categories: Programming, PHP

Id: 2
Title: What is PHP?
Author: Rita Chouhan
Categories: Programming, PHP

Id: 8
Title: Sphinx search engine
Author: Amit Badkas
Categories: Programming, Search
```

As expected, we got posts with ids **5,2**, and **8**. All these posts contain either "php" or "programming" or both.

Next, we tried our hand at SPH_MATCH_PHRASE, which returns only those records that match the search phrase exactly, that is, all words in the search phrase appear in the same order and consecutively in the index:

```
// Set the mode to SPH_MATCH_PHRASE
$client->SetMatchMode(SPH_MATCH_PHRASE);

display_results(
    $client->Query('php programming'),
    '"php programming" with SPH_MATCH_PHRASE');

display_results(
    $client->Query('scripting language'),
    '"scripting language" with SPH_MATCH_PHRASE');
```

The previous two function calls return the following results:

"php programming" with SPH_MATCH_PHRASE

No results found

"scripting language" with SPH_MATCH_PHRASE

Id: 2
Title: What is PHP?
Author: Rita Chouhan
Categories: Programming, PHP

The query"php programming" didn't return any results because there were no posts that match that exact phrase. However, a post with id **2** matched the next query: "scripting language".

The last matching mode we used was SPH_MATCH_FULLSCAN. When this mode is used the search phrase is completely ignored, (in our case "php" was ignored) and Sphinx returns all records from the index:

```
// Set the mode to SPH_MATCH_FULLSCAN
$client->SetMatchMode(SPH_MATCH_FULLSCAN);

display_results(
    $client->Query('php'),
    '"php programming" with SPH_MATCH_FULLSCAN');
```

The function call returns the following result (for brevity only a part of the output is shown in the following image):

"php programming" with SPH_MATCH_FULLSCAN

Id: 1
Title: Electronics For You
Author: Aditya Mooley
Categories: Programming, Games, Electronics

Id: 2
Title: What is PHP?
Author: Rita Chouhan
Categories: Programming, PHP

Id: 3
Title: Nintendo
Author: Dr.Tarique Sani
Categories: Games, Electronics

 SPH_MATCH_FULLSCAN mode is automatically used if empty string is passed to the SphinxClient::Query() method.

SPH_MATCH_FULLSCAN matches all indexed documents, but the search query still applies all the filters when sorting and grouping. However, the search query will not perform any full-text searching. This is particularly useful in cases where we only want to apply filters and don't want to perform any full-text matching (For example, filtering all blog posts by categories).

Boolean query syntax

Boolean mode queries allow expressions to make use of a complex set of Boolean rules to refine their searches. These queries are very powerful when applied to full-text searching. When using Boolean query syntax, certain characters have special meaning, as given in the following list:

- **&**: Explicit AND operator
- **|**: OR operator
- **-**: NOT operator
- **!**: NOT operator (alternate)
- **()**: Grouping

Let's try to understand each of these operators using an example.

Time for action – searching using Boolean query syntax

1. Create a PHP script `search_boolean_mode.php` in your webroot with the following code:

```php
<?php
// Include the api class
require_once('sphinxapi.php');
// Include the file which contains the function to display results
require_once('display_results.php');

$client = new SphinxClient();
// Set search options
$client->SetServer('localhost', 9312);
$client->SetConnectTimeout(1);
$client->SetArrayResult(true);

display_results(
$client->Query('php programming'),
'"php programming" (default mode)');

// Set the mode to SPH_MATCH_BOOLEAN
$client->SetMatchMode(SPH_MATCH_BOOLEAN);

// Search using AND operator
display_results(
$client->Query('php & programming'),
'"php & programming"');

// Search using OR operator
display_results(
$client->Query('php | programming'),
'"php | programming"');

// Search using NOT operator
display_results(
$client->Query('php -programming'),
'"php -programming"');

// Search by grouping terms
display_results(
$client->Query('(php & programming) | (leadership & success)'),
'"(php & programming) | (leadership & success)"');
```

```
// Demonstrate how OR precedence is higher than AND
display_results(
$client->Query('development framework | language'),
'"development framework | language"');

// This won't work
display_results($client->Query('-php'), '"-php"');
```

Execute the script in a browser (the output shown in next section).

What just happened?

We created a PHP script to see how different Boolean operators work. Let's understand the working of each of them.

The first search query, "php programming", did not use any operator. There is always an implicit AND operator, so "php programming" query actually means: "php & programming". In second search query we explicitly used the & (AND) operator. Thus the output of both the queries were exactly same, as shown in the following screenshot:

"php programming" (default mode)

Id: 5
Title: Namespaces in PHP 5.3
Author: Aditya Mooley
Categories: Programming, PHP

"php & programming"

Id: 5
Title: Namespaces in PHP 5.3
Author: Aditya Mooley
Categories: Programming, PHP

Our third search query used the OR operator. If either of the terms get matched whilst using OR, the document is returned. Thus "php | programming" will return all documents that match either "php" or "programming", as seen in the following screenshot:

```
"php | programming"

Id: 2
Title: What is PHP?
Author: Rita Chouhan
Categories: Programming, PHP
```

```
Id: 5
Title: Namespaces in PHP 5.3
Author: Aditya Mooley
Categories: Programming, PHP
```

```
Id: 8
Title: Sphinx search engine
Author: Amit Badkas
Categories: Programming, Search
```

The fourth search query used the NOT operator. In this case, the word that comes just after the NOT operator should not be present in the matched results. So `"php -programming"` will return all documents that match "php" but do not match "programming" We get results as seen in the following screenshot:

```
"php -programming"

Id: 2
Title: What is PHP?
Author: Rita Chouhan
Categories: Programming, PHP
```

Next, we used the grouping operator. This operator is used to group other operators. We searched for `"(php & programming) | (leadership & success)"`, and this returned all documents which matched either; "php" and "programming" or "leadership" and "success", as seen in the next screenshot:

```
"(php & programming) | (leadership & success)"

Id: 5
Title: Namespaces in PHP 5.3
Author: Aditya Mooley
Categories: Programming, PHP
```

```
Id: 6
Title: Leadership Skills
Author: Aditya Mooley
Categories: Misc
```

After that, we fired a query to see how OR has a precedence higher than AND. The query "development framework | language" is treated by Sphinx as "(development) & (framework | language)". Hence we got documents matching "development & framework" and "development & language", as shown here:

> **"development framework | language"**
>
> Id: 2
> Title: What is PHP?
> Author: Rita Chouhan
> Categories: Programming, PHP

Lastly, we saw how a query like "-php" does not return anything. Ideally it should have returned all documents which do not match "php", but for technical and performance reasons such a query is not evaluated. When this happens we get the following output:

> **"-php"**
>
> No results found

Extended query syntax

Apart from the Boolean operators, there are some more specialized operators and modifiers that can be used when using the extended matching mode.

Let's understand this with an example.

Time for action – searching with extended query syntax

1. Create a PHP script search_extended_mode.php in your webroot with following code:

```php
<?php
// Include the api class
Require_once('sphinxapi.php');
// Include the file which contains the function to display results
Require_once('display_results.php');

$client = new SphinxClient();
// Set search options
$client->SetServer('localhost', 9312);
$client->SetConnectTimeout(1);
$client->SetArrayResult(true);
```

```
// Set the mode to SPH_MATCH_EXTENDED2
$client->SetMatchMode(SPH_MATCH_EXTENDED2);

// Returns documents whose title matches "php" and
// content matches "significant"
display_results(
$client->Query('@title php @content significant'),
'field search operator');

// Returns documents where "development" comes
// before 8th position in content field
display_results(
$client->Query('@content[8] development'),
'field position limit modifier');

// Returns only those documents where both title and content
// matches "php" and "namespaces"
display_results(
$client->Query('@(title,content) php namespaces'),
'multi-field search operator');

// Returns documents where any of the field
// matches "games"
display_results(
$client->Query('@* games'),
'all-field search operator');

// Returns documents where "development framework"
// phrase matches exactly
display_results(
$client->Query('"development framework"'),
'phrase search operator');

// Returns documents where there are three words
// between "people" and "passion"
display_results(
$client->Query('"people passion"~3'),
'proximity search operator');

// Returns documents where any of the
// two words from the phrase matches
display_results(
$client->Query('"people development passion framework"/2'),
'quorum search operator');
```

2. Execute the script in a browser (the output is explained in the next section).

What just happened?

For using extended query syntax, we set the match mode to SPH_MATCH_EXTENDED2:

```
$client->SetMatchMode(SPH_MATCH_EXTENDED2);
```

The first operator we used was **field search operator**. Using this operator we can tell Sphinx which fields to search against (instead of searching against all fields). In our example we searched for all documents whose title matches "php" and whose content matches "significant". As an output, we got posts (documents) with the id **5,** which was the only document that satisfied this matching condition as shown below:

```
@title php @content significant
```

The search for that term returns the following result:

> **field search operator**
>
> Id: 5
> Title: Namespaces in PHP 5.3
> Author: Aditya Mooley
> Categories: Programming, PHP

Following this we used **field position limit modifier**. The modifier instructs Sphinx to select only those documents where "development" comes before the 8th position in the content field, that is, it limits the search to the first eight positions within given field.

```
@content[8] development
```

And we get the following result:

> **field position limit modifier**
>
> Id: 7
> Title: Ruby on Rails
> Author: Dr.Tarique Sani
> Categories: Programming

Next, we used the **multiple field search operator**. With this operator you can specify which fields (combined) should match the queried terms. In our example, documents are only matched when both title and content matches "php" and "namespaces".

```
@(title,content) php namespaces
```

This gives the following result:

```
all-field search operator

Id: 3
Title: Nintendo
Author: Dr.Tarique Sani
Categories: Games, Electronics
```

The **all-field search operator** was used next. In this case the query is matched against all fields.

```
@* games
```

This search term gives the following result:

```
all-field search operator

Id: 3
Title: Nintendo
Author: Dr.Tarique Sani
Categories: Games, Electronics
```

The **phrase search operator** works exactly same as when we set the matching mode to SPH_MATCH_PHRASE. This operator implicitly does the same. So, a search for the phrase "development framework" returns posts with id **7,** since the exact phrase appears in its content.

```
"development framework"
```

The search term returns the following result:

```
phrase search operator

Id: 7
Title: Ruby on Rails
Author: Dr.Tarique Sani
Categories: Programming
```

Next we used the **proximity search operator**. The proximity distance is specified in words, adjusted for word count, and applies to all words within quotes. So, `"people passion"~3` means there must be a span of less than five words that contain both the words "people" and "passion". We get the following result:

---
proximity search operator

Id: 1
Title: Electronics For You
Author: Aditya Mooley
Categories: Programming, Games, Electronics

The last operator we used is called as a **quorum operator**. In this, Sphinx returns only those documents that match the given threshold of words. `"people development passion framework"/2` matches those documents where at least two words match out of the four words in the query. Our query returns the following result:

---
quorum search operator

Id: 7
Title: Ruby on Rails
Author: Dr.Tarique Sani
Categories: Programming

Id: 1
Title: Electronics For You
Author: Aditya Mooley
Categories: Programming, Games, Electronics

Using what we have learnt above, you can create complex search queries by combining any of the previously listed search operators. For example:

```
@title programming "photo gallery" -(asp|jsp) @* opensource
```

The query means that:

- The document's title field should match 'programming'
- The same document must also contain the words 'photo' and 'gallery' adjacently in any of the fields
- The same document must not contain the words 'asp' or 'jsp'
- The same document must contain the word 'opensource' in any of its fields

There are few more operators in extended query syntax and you can see their examples at `http://sphinxsearch.com/docs/manual-0.9.9.html#extended-syntax`.

Filtering full-text search results

In most cases, full-text searching alone didn't serve our purpose. We had to filter the results based on the document attributes. For example, when searching blog posts, you might want to provide a filter wherein only posts from a certain category are returned. In such scenarios the result filtering methods of the client API comes handy. Let's take a look.

Time for action – filtering the result set

1. Create a PHP script `search_filter.php` in your webroot containing the following code:

```php
<?php
// Include the api class
Require_once('sphinxapi.php');
// Include the file which contains the function to display results
Require_once('display_results.php');

$client = new SphinxClient();

$client->SetServer('localhost', 9312);
$client->SetConnectTimeout(1);
$client->SetArrayResult(true);

$client->SetMatchMode(SPH_MATCH_ANY);
// Returns all documents which match "programming games
electronics"
display_results(
$client->Query('programming games electronics'),
'all posts matching "programming games electronics"');

// Filter by ID
$client->SetIDRange(1, 4);

// Same as above but with ID based filtering
display_results(
$client->Query('programming games electronics'),
'above query with ID based filtering');

// Reset the ID based filter
$client->SetIDRange(0, 0);

// Filter the posts by author's Aditya Mooley and Dr.Tarique Sani
$client->SetFilter('author_id', array(2, 4));
```

```
display_results(
$client->Query('programming games electronics'),
'posts filtered by author');

// Filter the posts by category Games
$client->SetFilter('category_id', array(2));
display_results(
$client->Query('programming games electronics'),
'posts filtered by categories');

// Filter the posts by publish_date using range filter
$client->SetFilterRange(
'publish_date',
strtotime('2010-01-01'),
strtotime('2010-01-30'));

display_results(
$client->Query('programming games electronics'),
'posts filtered publish date range');
```

2. Run the script in a browser (the output is explained in the next section).

What just happened?

We used the Sphinx client API's filtering methods to filter our search results. In all our above queries we searched for the same set of terms, such as "programming games electronics", but with different filters.

The first search query returned all results without any filtering. Before issuing the second search query we used the SetIDRange($min, $max) method. This method filters out the results based on the minimum and maximum ID values passed to it. So in our case we only got those documents whose ID were in between one and four. The un-filtered and filtered results are as shown in the following screenshot:

```
all posts matching "programming games electronics"

Id: 1
Title: Electronics For You
Author: Aditya Mooley
Categories: Programming, Games, Electronics

Id: 3
Title: Nintendo
Author: Dr.Tarique Sani
Categories: Games, Electronics

Id: 5
Title: Namespaces in PHP 5.3
Author: Aditya Mooley
Categories: Programming, PHP

Id: 8
Title: Sphinx search engine
Author: Amit Badkas
Categories: Programming, Search

above query with ID based filtering

Id: 1
Title: Electronics For You
Author: Aditya Mooley
Categories: Programming, Games, Electronics

Id: 3
Title: Nintendo
Author: Dr.Tarique Sani
Categories: Games, Electronics
```

After that, we reset our ID range filter by passing 0 as minimum and maximum values. We then filtered our search results by author. We filtered them so that we only get posts by Aditya Mooley (author_id 2) and Dr.Tarique Sani (author_id 4).

```
$client->SetFilter('author_id', array(2, 4));
```

The filter returns the following result:

```
posts filtered by author

Id: 1
Title: Electronics For You
Author: Aditya Mooley
Categories: Programming, Games, Electronics

Id: 3
Title: Nintendo
Author: Dr.Tarique Sani
Categories: Games, Electronics

Id: 5
Title: Namespaces in PHP 5.3
Author: Aditya Mooley
Categories: Programming, PHP
```

`SetFilter($attribute, $values, $exclude=false)` takes three parameters. The first is the attribute on which the filtering should be done. The second is an array of integer values to be filtered, meaning documents matching any of these values will be returned. The third parameter is an optional Boolean parameter, and if passed as `true` will actually exclude the values passed, instead of including them.

Next we filtered results based on `category_id`, which is an MVA. Filtering on normal and MVA attributes works in a similar fashion, as far as calling the `SetFilter()` method is concerned. If the attribute is MVA, then it matches all those documents where any of the values stored in the MVA field matches any of the passed values. The filter returns the following result:

---

posts filtered by categories

Id: 1
Title: Electronics For You
Author: Aditya Mooley
Categories: Programming, Games, Electronics

Id: 3
Title: Nintendo
Author: Dr.Tarique Sani
Categories: Games, Electronics

We previously searched for all posts that are in category 'Games' (`category_id` 2). Since `category_id` is an MVA, it holds multiple values, and if any of those values matches 2 then that document is returned.

The filter set for author was not reset when we filtered by category, and hence both the filters were applied. The results were filtered by author as well as category. So our final result returned those posts whose author is either *Aditya Mooley* or *Dr.Tarique Sani*, and whose category is *Games*.

To filter the results based on a range of values we used the `SetFilterRange($attribute, $min, $max, $exclude=false)` method. All parameters are self explanatory. We filtered our search results so that we only get those posts that were published between 1st January 2010 and 30th January 2010.

```
$client->SetFilterRange('publish_date', strtotime('2010-01-01'),
strtotime('2010-01-30'));
```

The ranged filter returned the following result:

```
posts filtered publish date range

Id: 3
Title: Nintendo
Author: Dr.Tarique Sani
Categories: Games, Electronics
```

There are more methods available to filter search results:

♦ `SetFilterFloatRange ( $attribute, $min, $max, $exclude=false )` —Works similar to `SetFilterRange()` but for float range values

♦ `SetGeoAnchor ( $attrlat, $attrlong, $lat, $long )` —Used for filtering based on geolocation (explained in later chapters)

Weighting search results

Weighting decides which document gets priority over other documents and appear at the top. In Sphinx, weighting depends on the search mode. Weight can also be referred to as ranking. There are two major parts which are used in weighting functions:

♦ **Phrase rank**: This is based on the length of **Longest Common Subsequence (LCS)** of search words between document body and query phrase. This means that the documents in which the queried phrase matches perfectly will have a higher phrase rank and the weight would be equal to the query word counts.

♦ **Statistical rank**: This is based on BM25 function which takes only the frequency of the queried words into account. So, if a word appears only one time in the whole document then its weight will be low. On the other hand if a word appears a lot in the document then its weight will be higher. The **BM25 weight** is a floating point number between 0 and 1.

Time for action – weighting search results

1. Modify `display_results.php` (created earlier) and add the code as highlighted next:

```
if (count($cats)) {
    print "<br />Categories: " . implode(', ', $cats);
}
print "<br />Weight: " . $result['weight'];
print "<hr />";
```

2. Create a PHP script `search_weighting.php` in your webroot containing the following code:

```php
<?php
// Include the api class
require('sphinxapi.php');
// Include the file which contains the function to display results
require_once('display_results.php');

$client = new SphinxClient();

$client->SetServer('localhost', 9312);
$client->SetConnectTimeout(1);
$client->SetArrayResult(true);

$client->SetMatchMode(SPH_MATCH_ANY);
display_results(
$client->Query('php language framework'),
'MATCH ANY');

$client->SetMatchMode(SPH_MATCH_BOOLEAN);
display_results(
$client->Query('php | framework'),
'BOOLEAN');

$client->SetMatchMode(SPH_MATCH_EXTENDED2);
display_results(
$client->Query('@* php | @* framework'),
'EXTENDED');
```

3. Execute the script in a browser.

What just happened?

We added code to show the weight in `display_results.php`. We then created a script to see how the weights are calculated when different matching modes are used.

In all modes, per-field weighted phrase ranks are computed as a product of LCS and per-field weight is specified by the user. The default value of per-field weight is 1 and they are always integer. They can never be less than 1.

 You can use `SetFieldWeights($weights)` API method to set per-field weight. `$weights` should be an associative array mapping string field names to integer value.

When SPH_MATCH_ANY is used, Sphinx adds a count of matching words in each field and before that weighted phrase ranks are additionally multiplied by a value big enough to guarantee that higher rank in any field will make the match ranked higher, even if it's field weight is low.

SPH_MATCH_BOOLEAN is a special case, wherein no weighting is performed at all and every match weight is set to 1.

The last mode we saw was SPH_MATCH_EXTENDED2, in which the final weight is a sum of weighted phrase ranks and BM25 weight. This sum is then multiplied by 1,000 and rounded to an integer. This is shown in the following screenshot:

EXTENDED

Id: 5
Title: Namespaces in PHP 5.3
Author: Aditya Mooley
Categories: Programming, PHP
Weight: 2601

Id: 2
Title: What is PHP?
Author: Rita Chouhan
Categories: Programming, PHP
Weight: 2589

Id: 7
Title: Ruby on Rails
Author: Dr.Tarique Sani
Categories: Programming
Weight: 1647

Sphinx's motto is to present results with better sub-phrase matches, and perfect matches are pulled to the top.

 At the time of writing this book ranking mode can be explicitly set for SPH_MATCH_EXTENDED2 matching mode using the SetRankingMode() API method.

Sorting modes

At times you might want to sort the results by values other than relevance. The Sphinx API provides `SetSortMode($mode, $sortby="")` method which can be used to set the sort mode other than relevance, which is the default sort mode.

The following sorting modes are available in Sphinx:

- `SPH_SORT_RELEVANCE`: Sorts by relevance in descending order, that is, best matches first
- `SPH_SORT_ATTR_DESC`: Sorts by an attribute in descending order, that is, bigger attribute values first
- `SPH_SORT_ATTR_ASC`: Same as `SPH_SORT_ATTR_DESC`, but sorts in ascending order
- `SPH_SORT_TIME_SEGMENTS`: Sorts by time segments (last hour/day/week/month), in descending order, and then by relevance in descending order
- `SPH_SORT_EXTENDED`: Sorts by SQL-like combination in `ASC` or `DESC` order
- `SPH_SORT_EXPR`: Sorts by an arithmetic expression

Examples:

```
// Sort by relevance. Second parameter is not required in this case.
$client->SetSortMode(SPH_SORT_RELEVANCE);

// Sort by author_id in descending order
$client->SetSortMode(SPH_SORT_ATTR_DESC, 'author_id');

// Sort by time segments i.e. first the results
// will be sorted based on publish date and then on relevance.
$client->SetSortMode(SPH_SORT_TIME_SEGMENTS, 'publish_date');

// Extended sort: Sort by weight desc and id asc which
// is same as sorting by relevance
$client->SetSortMode(SPH_SORT_EXTENDED, '@weight DESC, @id ASC');

// Sort by category_id desc and weight asc
$client->SetSortMode(SPH_SORT_EXTENDED, 'category_id DESC @weight
ASC');
```

Grouping search results

At times we may need to group our search results by an attribute. For example, to show monthly statistics about our blog posts we will need to group the posts by `publish_date`, or to show count of books by a particular author we will need to group the search results by author.

Sphinx offers a grouping mode which is enabled with `SetGroupBy()` API call. All matches are assigned to different groups based on group-by value when grouping is used.

Different functions are available to compute the group-by value:

- `SPH_GROUPBY_DAY`: Extracts year, month, and day in YYYYMMDD format from the `timestamp` attribute
- `SPH_GROUPBY_WEEK`: Extracts year and first day of the week number in YYYYNNN format from `timestamp`
- `SPH_GROUPBY_MONTH`: Extracts year and month in YYYYMM format from `timestamp`
- `SPH_GROUPBY_YEAR`: Extracts year in YYYY format from `timestamp`
- `SPH_GROUPBY_ATTR`: Attribute value is used for grouping

The function to be used for grouping is:

```
SetGroupBy ( $attribute, $func, $groupsort="@group desc" )
```

The first parameter is the attribute name on which the grouping should be done. The second parameter is the function grouping order to be used (one of the name mentioned above). And finally, the third parameter is a clause that controls how the groups will be sorted. Its syntax is similar to that shown in the example for the `SPH_SORT_EXTENDED` sorting mode earlier. The third parameter is optional.

The final search result set contains one best match per group. Grouping function value and per-group match count are returned as long as attributes names `@groupby` and `@count` respectively.

Example:

```
$client->SetMatchMode(SPH_MATCH_ANY);
$client->SetGroupBy('author_id', SPH_GROUPBY_ATTR);
$results = $client->Query('php language framework games electronics');

print_r($results);
```

The output of the script can be seen in the following screenshot:

```
[matches] => Array
    (
        [0] => Array
            (
                [id] => 3
                [weight] => 1
                [attrs] => Array
                    (
                        [publish_date] => 1262668161
                        [author_id] => 4
                        [category_id] => Array
                            (
                                [0] => 2
                                [1] => 3
                            )

                        [@groupby] => 4
                        [@count] => 2
                    )

            )

        [1] => Array
```

Summary

With the index (that we created in *Chapter 3*, *Indexing* as a base), in this chapter:

- ◆ We wrote different search queries
- ◆ We saw how PHP's implementation of the Sphinx client API can be used in PHP applications to issue some powerful search queries
- ◆ We also saw how to filter our search results by different attributes
- ◆ Lastly, we saw how to rank, sort, and group the search results by different attributes

In the next chapter we will build a practical application from the ground up, which will involve search using Sphinx.

5
Feed Search

I hope the earlier chapters got you warmed up and laid a solid foundation so that you can add a rock solid, fast, and accurate search engine to your applications.

In this chapter we will create our first functional application, which will use the Sphinx search engine as the backend to service search queries. We will start from scratch and build the complete application in PHP.

In this chapter we shall:

- ◆ Create a form to **add feed** title and its URL
- ◆ Create a Sphinx configuration file with **xmlpipe2 data source**
- ◆ Create a PHP script to **fetch the feed items** and output the XML to the Sphinx indexer
- ◆ Create a **search form** to input query and display the search results

So let's get on with it...

The application

First, let's understand what we are going to accomplish in this chapter. We will create an application wherein you can add feed URLs. These feeds will then be periodically fetched and indexed using Sphinx.

We will create some MySQL database tables to store feed information. However, we will not store the description of feed items in our database. The description will be stored in a Sphinx index so that full-text search queries can be issued against the index.

We will then create search form wherein a user can enter a search phrase, author, and also select multiple categories. On submission of the form we will perform a search on the Sphinx index and filter the results as per the categories selected.

The search results (feed items) will then be shown in the ascending order of relevance.

Tools and software used while creating this application

- PHP 5.3.2
- Apache 2.2.14
- MySQL 5.1.14
- Sphinx 0.9.9
- phpMyAdmin (to manage database)
- Ubuntu 10.04 LTS
- Firefox 3.6
- SimplePie version 1.2+

It is not mandatory that you should use the exact same version of the software listed here, although you should have PHP 5.x+.

 It is assumed that the reader has a basic knowledge of HTML, CSS, and PHP. It is beyond the scope of this book to explain the code written in HTML and PHP.

Database structure

The first thing we need to do is create the database to be used by the application. We will also need to chalk out and create the different tables that will be needed. Let's do it.

Time for action – creating the MySQL database and tables

1. Open phpMyAdmin and create a database **sphinx_feeds**. You can use an existing database as well.

2. Import the following SQL to create the database tables:

```
CREATE TABLE `categories` (
  `id` int(11) NOT NULL AUTO_INCREMENT,
  `name` varchar(100) NOT NULL,
  PRIMARY KEY (`id`),
  UNIQUE KEY `name` (`name`)
) ENGINE=MyISAM  DEFAULT CHARSET=utf8;
```

```
CREATE TABLE `feeds` (
  `id` int(11) NOT NULL AUTO_INCREMENT,
  `name` varchar(255) NOT NULL,
  `url` varchar(255) NOT NULL,
  `last_modified` datetime DEFAULT NULL,
  PRIMARY KEY (`id`)
) ENGINE=MyISAM  DEFAULT CHARSET=utf8;

CREATE TABLE `items` (
  `id` int(11) NOT NULL AUTO_INCREMENT,
  `title` varchar(255) NOT NULL,
  `guid` varchar(32) NOT NULL,
  `link` varchar(255) NOT NULL,
  `pub_date` datetime NOT NULL,
  PRIMARY KEY (`id`),
  UNIQUE KEY `guid` (`guid`)
) ENGINE=MyISAM  DEFAULT CHARSET=utf8;
```

What just happened?

We created a new database which will be used by our PHP application. We then created the following tables:

- ◆ categories: This table will hold the category names. A category is a collection of items sharing common attributes. Each item in the feed has one or more category assigned to it. New categories will get added to this table as and when they are found in the feed items. The data stored in this table will be used to populate the select box which, will be used for filtering the search results by categories.

- ◆ feeds: This table will store the feed URLs. While indexing, we will query this table to fetch all feed URLs whose data needs to be fetched and indexed.

- ◆ items: This table will store the feed items, that is, title and link. We will display the item titles in the search results.

The following screenshots demonstrate how each of the tables will be created:

categories:

Field	Type	Collation	Attributes	Null	Default	Extra
id	int(11)			No	*None*	auto_increment
name	varchar(100)	utf8_general_ci		No	*None*	

feeds:

Field	Type	Collation	Attributes	Null	Default	Extra
id	int(11)			No	*None*	auto_increment
name	varchar(255)	utf8_general_ci		No	*None*	
url	varchar(255)	utf8_general_ci		No	*None*	
last_modified	datetime			Yes	*NULL*	

items:

Field	Type	Collation	Attributes	Null	Default	Extra
id	int(11)			No	*None*	auto_increment
title	varchar(255)	utf8_general_ci		No	*None*	
guid	varchar(32)	utf8_general_ci		No	*None*	
link	varchar(255)	utf8_general_ci		No	*None*	
pub_date	datetime			No	*None*	

Basic setup

Lets create the directory that will hold our application files and other dependencies, such as the Sphinx API class and SimplePie feed parser. We will also be creating a few scripts that will act as helpers in our application and will contain some common code re-used throughout the application.

Time for action – setting up the feeds application

1. Create a directory `feeds` in your webroot, that is, `/path/to/webroot/feeds`:

   ```
   $ mkdir /path/to/webroot/feeds
   ```

2. Create the `/path/to/webroot/feeds/views` directory:

   ```
   $ mkdir /path/to/webroot/feeds/views
   ```

3. Copy the `sphinxapi.php` file from the Sphinx source directory to the `feeds` directory:

   ```
   $ cp /path/to/sphinx-0.9.9/api/sphinxapi.php /path/to/webroot/feeds/
   ```

4. Get the latest version of **SimplePie** RSS parser from `http://simplepie.org/`, extract the archive in any directory of your file system and copy the `simplepie.inc` file from the extracted archive to the `/path/to/webroot/feeds` directory:

```
$ cp /path/to/simplepie/simplepie.inc /path/to/webroot/feeds/
```

5. Create the file `/path/to/webroot/feeds/init.php` with the following code:

```php
<?php
/**
 * File: /path/to/webroot/feeds/init.php
 */
// Database connection credentials
$dsn  ='mysql:dbname=sphinx_feeds;host=localhost';
$user = 'root';
$pass = '';
// Instantiate the PDO (PHP 5 specific) class
try {
    $dbh = new PDO($dsn, $user, $pass);
} catch (PDOException $e){
    echo'Connection failed: '.$e->getMessage();
}


// Array to hold variables to be used in views
$viewVars = array();


/**
 * Method to fetch the contents of a view (THTML) file and return
the contents.
 * The html string returned by this method is then placed in the
master layout.
 *
 * @param string $view Name of the view file to be fetched and
parsed.
 *
 * @return string HTML contents specific to the passed view
 */
function get_view($view)
{
  global $viewVars;
  // Start the output buffering so that the html output of the
view is not sent
  // to the browser immediately.
  ob_start();
  // Include the view file which outputs the HTML
  include("views/$view.thtml");
```

```
      // Get the view contents in a variable i.e. whatever the above
view outputs,
      // it gets stored in a variable
      $contents = ob_get_contents();
      // Clean the buffer
      ob_end_clean();
      return $contents;
}//end get_view()


/**
 * Method to render the page.
 * This method along with get_view() acts as a very simple
templating
 * engine and separates the view logic from our php (business)
logic.
 *
 * @param string $view Name of the view file to be rendered
 */
function render($view)
{
   $contents = get_view($view);
   include('views/layout.thtml');
}//end render()
```

What just happened?

We created a project folder at /path/to/webroot/feeds. This will be our base directory, and will hold all files or directories related to our 'Feed Search' project.

After that we created the /path/to/webroot/feeds/views directory. This directory will hold our application's HTML template files. We will be creating these template files as we progress through this chapter.

We then copied the PHP implementation class of the Sphinx client API to our working directory. This class will be used for searching from within the PHP script.

As we will be fetching feeds and indexing its data, we will need to parse the feed RSS XML. For this we will use a third-party open source library called SimplePie. We downloaded the library and extracted its archive. We copied simplepie.inc to our working directory.

Lastly, we created a PHP script, /path/to/webroot/feeds/init.php, which will be included in all other PHP scripts. This script initializes the database connection and also contains a few methods used to render the HTML output.

We are going to use PHP 5's PDO class for database interaction.

The structure of your working directory (`/path/to/webroot/feeds`) will look like this:

```
feeds/
|-- init.php
|-- simplepie.inc
|-- sphinxapi.php
`-- views
```

Add feed

Let's move forward and create a form to add feed URLs. The form will ask the user for a feed title and feed URL.

Time for action – creating a form to add feeds

1. Create the master layout at `/path/to/webroot/feeds/views/layout.thtml`:

```html
<!-- File: /path/to/webroot/feeds/views/layout.thtml -->
<!DOCTYPE html PUBLIC "-//W3C//DTD XHTML 1.0 Transitional//EN"
    "http://www.w3.org/TR/xhtml1/DTD/xhtml1-transitional.dtd"><html>
<head>
<title>Feed Search</title>
<link rel="stylesheet" type="text/css" href="style.css" />
</head>
<body>
  <div id="header">
    <h1>Feed search using Sphinx</h1>
  </div>
  <div id="nav">
    <ul>
      <li><a href="search.php">Search</a></li>
      <li><a href="add.php">Add Feed</a></li>
    </ul>
  </div>
  <div id="content">
    <?php echo $contents; ?>
  </div>
</body>
</html>
```

2. Create `/path/to/webroot/feeds/style.css`:

```css
/** File: /path/to/webroot/feeds/style.css **/
body {
  font-family: verdana,arial,sans-serif;
  font-size: 12px;
  margin: 0;
  overflow: auto;
}
#header {
  text-align: center;
  background-color: #606060;
  color: #ffffff;
  height: 70px;
  padding-top: 5px;
}
#nav ul {
  list-style: none;
  padding: 5px;
  margin: 0px;
}
#nav ul li {
  display: inline;
  padding: 5px 10px 5px 10px;
  border-right: 1px solid;
}
#nav {
  background-color: #000000;
  color: #ffffff;
}
#nav a {
  color: #ffffff;
  text-decoration: none;
  font-weight: bold;
}
#content {
  padding: 10px;
}
div.input {
  padding: 5px;
}
label {
  width: 100px;
  text-align: right;
```

```
  display: block;
  float: left;
}
.information {
  color: #28630B;
}
```

3. Create a file /path/to/webroot/feeds/add.php with the following content:

```php
<?php
/**
 * File: /path/to/webroot/feeds/add.php
 */
include('init.php');

// If we have data in POST then get it from there else initialize
// to empty strings
$viewVars['name'] = !empty($_POST['name']) ? $_POST['name'] : '';
$viewVars['url']  = !empty($_POST['url']) ? $_POST['url'] : '';

// Render the view
render('add');
```

4. Create the view for the form at /path/to/webroot/feeds/views/add.thtml:

```html
<!-- File: /path/to/webroot/feeds/views/add.thtml -->
<form action="add.php" method="post">
  <fieldset>
    <legend>Add Feed</legend>
    <div class="input">
      <label>Feed Name: </label>
      <input type="text" name="name"
        value="<?php echo $viewVars['name']; ?>" />
    </div>
    <div class="input">
      <label>Feed Url: </label>
      <input type="text" name="url"
        value="<?php echo $viewVars['url']; ?>" />
    </div>
    <div class="input">
      <label> </label>
      <input type="submit" name="submit" value="Add" />
    </div>
  </fieldset>
</form>
```

5. Open `add.php` in a browser (`http://localhost/feeds/add.php`).

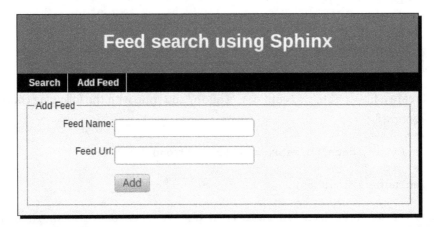

What just happened?

We first created a master HTML layout template for our application. All our pages will use this layout. We then added some CSS styles so that our web page looks pretty.

After that, we created our main script, `add.php`, which will be executed through a browser. We added code to include the init.php, which initiated the database connection, and to render the view that contains the HTML for form creation. In the form, we added two fields for the feed name and feed URL.

Saving the feed data

The form that we just created won't do anything when you submit it. Now let's add code to save the form's content to the **feeds** database table. While saving we will also check if a feed URL already exists in our database and reject the duplicates.

Time for action – adding code to save feed

1. Add the code to save form data in `/path/to/webroot/feeds/add.php` as shown in the following highlighted code:

```
<?php
/**
 * File: /path/to/webroot/feeds/add.php
 */
include('init.php');

// If we have data in POST then get it from there else initialize
```

```
        // to empty strings
        $viewVars['name'] = !empty($_POST['name']) ? $_POST['name'] : '';
        $viewVars['url']  = !empty($_POST['url']) ? $_POST['url'] : '';

        // Check if form is submitted and if we have a feed name and url
        // then save the data
        if (!empty($_POST['name']) && !empty($_POST['url'])) {
            // First check if the feed being added is already in our
               database
            $stmt = $dbh->prepare("SELECT id FROM feeds WHERE url = :url");
            $stmt->bindParam(':url', strip_tags(
                    $viewVars['url']),
                    PDO::PARAM_STR);
            $stmt->execute();
            $result = $stmt->fetch(PDO::FETCH_ASSOC);
           // If this is not a duplicate item then only add it
           if (empty($result)) {
             $stmt = $dbh->prepare("INSERT INTO feeds SET name = :name,
                    url = :url");
             $stmt->bindParam(':name', strip_tags($viewVars['name']),
                    PDO::PARAM_STR);
             $stmt->bindParam(':url', strip_tags($viewVars['url']),
                    PDO::PARAM_STR);
             $stmt->execute();
             $viewVars['success'] = true;
             $viewVars['name'] = '';
             $viewVars['url']  = '';
           } else {
             $viewVars['error'] = 'This feed has already been added';
           }
        }


        // Render the view
        render('add');
```

2. Modify the view file and add code to show the success message:

```
    <!-- File: /path/to/webroot/feeds/views/add.thtml -->
    <form action="add.php" method="post">
<?php if (!empty($viewVars['success'])): ?>
<div class="information">Feed saved successfully</div><br />
<?php endif; ?>
  <?php if (!empty($viewVars['error'])) : ?>
```

```
    <div class="error"><?php echo $viewVars['error']; ?></div><br
/>
    <?php endif; ?>
<fieldset>
  <legend>Add Feed</legend>
  <div class="input">
    <label>Feed Name: </label>
```

3. Open the `add.php` file in browser and enter the data as shown in the following screenshot (you may use any name and a valid feed URL).

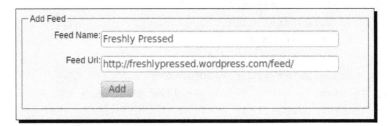

4. Click on **Add** to save the feed data.

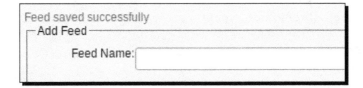

5. Similarly, add a few more feeds. I added the following:

- Packt Publishing—`http://www.packtpub.com/rss.xml`
- Drupal.org—`http://drupal.org/node/feed`
- Tech Crunch—`http://feeds.feedburner.com/TechCrunch`

What just happened?

In this exercise, we added the code to save the feed name and URL in the `feeds` database table. In `add.php` we checked if the form had been posted and then saved the data in the database.

If a feed is added to the database, a success message is shown above the form. This was done by modifying the `add.thtml` view and checking for the presence of a success variable.

Lastly, we did some data entry work by adding four different feeds.

If you now open your database (through phpMyAdmin), you will see that the data has been saved there:

id	name	url
1	Freshly Pressed	http://freshlypressed.wordpress.com/feed/
2	Packt Publications	http://www.packtpub.com/rss.xml
3	Drupal.org	http://drupal.org/node/feed
4	Tech Crunch	http://feeds.feedburner.com/TechCrunch

Indexing the feeds

Now that we have the feed URL saved in our database, let's create a script to fetch the feed items and put them in a Sphinx index.

Time for action – create the index

1. Create the Sphinx configuration file at `/usr/local/sphinx/etc/feeds.conf` with the following content:

```
source feeds
{
  type            = xmlpipe2
  xmlpipe_command = /usr/bin/php /path/to/webroot/feeds/
makeindex.php
  xmlpipe_field   = title
  xmlpipe_field   = description
  xmlpipe_field   = author
  xmlpipe_attr_timestamp = pub_date
  xmlpipe_attr_multi = category_id
}

index feed-items
{
  source        = feeds
  path          = /usr/local/sphinx/var/data/feed-items
  charset_type  = utf-8
}

indexer
{
  mem_limit     = 64M
}
```

2. Create the PHP script, `/path/to/webroot/feeds/makeindex.php`, to stream the XML required for indexing:

```php
<?php
require('init.php');
require('simplepie.inc');

// Instantiate the simplepie class
// We will use simplepie to parse the feed xml
$feed = new SimplePie();
// We don't want to cache feed items
$feed->enable_cache(false);
$feed->set_timeout(30);

// We will use PHP's inbuilt XMLWriter to create the xml structure
$xmlwriter = new XMLWriter();
$xmlwriter->openMemory();
$xmlwriter->setIndent(true);
$xmlwriter->startDocument('1.0', 'UTF-8');

// Start the parent docset element
$xmlwriter->startElement('sphinx:docset');

// Select all feeds from database
$query = "SELECT * FROM feeds";
$feeds = $dbh->query($query);

// Run a loop on all feeds and fetch the items
foreach ($feeds as $row) {
  // Fetch the feed
  $feed->set_feed_url($row['url']);
  $feed->init();

  // Fetch all items of this feed
  foreach ($feed->get_items() as $item) {
    $id = $item->get_id(true);
    $query = "INSERT INTO items (title, guid, link, pub_date)
VALUES (?, ?, ?, ?)";
    $stmt = $dbh->prepare();
    // Params to be binded in the sql
    $params = array(
            $item->get_title(),
            $id,
            $item->get_permalink(),
            $item->get_date('Y-m-d H;i:s'),
```

```php
    );
$stmt->execute($params);

// Start the element for holding the actual document (item)
$xmlwriter->startElement('sphinx:document');
// Add the id attribute which will be the id of the last
// record inserted in the items table.
$xmlwriter->writeAttribute("id", $dbh->lastInsertId());

// Set value for the title field
$xmlwriter->startElement('title');
$xmlwriter->text($item->get_title());
$xmlwriter->endElement();//end title

// Set value for the description field
$xmlwriter->startElement('description');
$xmlwriter->text($item->get_description());
$xmlwriter->endElement();// end description

// Set value for the author field
$xmlwriter->startElement('author');
// If we have the author name then get it
// else it will be empty string
if ($item->get_author()) {
  $author = $item->get_author()->get_name();
} else {
  $author = '';
}
$xmlwriter->text($author);
$xmlwriter->endElement();// end author

// Set value for the publish_date attribute
$xmlwriter->startElement('pub_date');
$xmlwriter->text($item->get_date('U'));
$xmlwriter->endElement();// end attribute

// Get all categories of this item
$categories = $item->get_categories();
$catIds = array();
// If we have categories then insert them in database
if ($categories) {
  // Insert the categories
  foreach ($item->get_categories() as $category) {
    $catName = $category->get_label();
```

```
            $stmt = $dbh->prepare(
              "INSERT INTO categories (name) VALUES (?)");
            $stmt->execute(array($catName));
            $catIds[] = $dbh->lastInsertId();
        }
      }

      // Set value for the category_id attribute
      // Multiple category ids should be comma separated
      $xmlwriter->startElement('category_id');
      $xmlwriter->text(implode(',', $catIds));
      $xmlwriter->endElement();// end attribute

      $xmlwriter->endElement();// end document
    }
  }
$xmlwriter->endElement();// end docset

// Output the xml
print $xmlwriter->flush();
```

3. Run the `indexer` command to create the index (as root):

   `$ /usr/local/sphinx/bin/indexer -c /usr/local/sphinx/etc/feeds.conf feed-items`

```
using config file '/usr/local/sphinx/etc/feeds.conf'...
indexing index 'feed-items'...
collected 110 docs, 0.1 MB
collected 213 attr values
sorted 0.0 Mvalues, 100.0% done
sorted 0.0 Mhits, 100.0% done
total 110 docs, 92506 bytes
total 0.052 sec, 1778619 bytes/sec, 2114.97 docs/sec
total 3 reads, 0.000 sec, 25.4 kb/call avg, 0.0 msec/call avg
total 9 writes, 0.001 sec, 21.4 kb/call avg, 0.1 msec/call avg
```

4. Test the index from the command line:

   `$ /usr/local/sphinx/bin/search -c /usr/local/sphinx/etc/feeds.conf development`

 You will get a different set of results depending on the feeds you added and the current items in those feeds.

```
using config file '/usr/local/sphinx/etc/feeds.conf'...
index 'feed-items': query 'development ': returned 7 matches of 7 total in 0.01

displaying matches:
1. document=41, weight=2, pub_date=Wed Sep 29 18:05:00 2010, category_id=()
2. document=25, weight=1, pub_date=Thu Sep 30 17:39:28 2010, category_id=()
3. document=26, weight=1, pub_date=Thu Sep 30 17:39:21 2010, category_id=()
4. document=67, weight=1, pub_date=Thu Sep 16 07:22:29 2010, category_id=(67)
5. document=74, weight=1, pub_date=Tue Aug 24 04:35:24 2010, category_id=(74)
6. document=85, weight=1, pub_date=Mon Jul 26 19:13:13 2010, category_id=(85)
7. document=86, weight=1, pub_date=Mon Oct  4 15:25:25 2010, category_id=(83,84

words:
1. 'development': 7 documents, 10 hits
```

What just happened?

As always, the first thing we did was to create the Sphinx configuration file. We defined the source, index, and indexer blocks with necessary options.

For indexing the feed items we will use the xmlpipe2 data source. We chose xmlpipe2 over an SQL data source because the data is coming from a non-conventional source (feed), and we do not store the feed items (description) in our database.

We defined the fields and attributes in the configuration file. The following fields and attributes will be created in the index:

- title: Full-text field to hold the title of the feed item
- description: Full-text field to hold the description of the feed item
- author: Full-text field to hold the author name
- pub_data: Timestamp attribute to hold the publish date of the feed item
- category_id: MVA attribute to hold categories associated with a feed item

The XML will be streamed by a PHP script, which we will create at /path/to/webroot/ feeds/makeindex.php. The index will be saved at /usr/local/sphinx/var/data/ feed-items.

After that, we created the PHP script makeindex.php, which streams the XML required by Sphinx to index the feed data. We used SimplePie to fetch the feeds and parse it into PHP objects so that we can loop over the data and save it in our database.

In makeindex.php, we wrote code to fetch all feed URLs stored in the feeds database table and then fetch each feed one by one. We are storing the feed title, guid (unique identifier for the item and comes along with the item in the feed XML), and link in the items table. We need to do this to show the feed title and link in our search results page.

We are also storing the data: categories associated with the items. We will need the category names to build the drop-down on a search page (for filtering purposes).

Apart from storing the data in the database, we also created the XML structure and data, as required by Sphinx, to create the index. This XML is then flushed at the end of the script.

Everything looks fine—right? Well there is one flaw in our PHP script which streams the XML. We are going to run the `indexer` once everyday to fetch feed items. However, what if the same items are returned on consecutive runs? What if the same category name is being used by different items? We certainly don't want to duplicate the data. Let's see how to rectify this.

Check for duplicate items

Let's modify the file which streams the XML and add code so that it doesn't include an item in the XML that has already been indexed. For this we will use the unique `guid` field and before considering it for indexing, check if an item with the same `guid` already exists in the items table. Let's do it.

Time for action – adding code to avoid duplicate items

Modify `/path/to/webroot/feeds/makeindex.php` and add the following code (only the concerned portion of code is shown for brevity):

```php
// Run a loop on all feeds and fetch the items
foreach ($feeds as $row) {
  // Fetch the feed
  $feed->set_feed_url($row['url']);
  $feed->init();

  // Fetch all items of this feed
  foreach ($feed->get_items() as $item) {
    $id = $item->get_id(true);

    // Check if an item with same id (guid) exists in our database
    $stmt = $dbh->prepare("SELECT id FROM items WHERE guid = ?");
    $stmt->execute(array($id));
    // If the item already exists
    // we will skip it and continue to the next item
    if ($stmt->rowCount()) {
    continue;
    }

      $query = "INSERT INTO items (title, guid, link, pub_date)
```

```
VALUES (?, ?, ?, ?)";
$stmt = $dbh->prepare($query);
// Params to be binded in the sql

// If we have categories then insert them in database
if ($categories) {
  // Insert the categories
  foreach ($item->get_categories() as $category) {
    $catName = $category->get_label();

  // Check if this category already exists
   $query = "SELECT id FROM categories WHERE name = ?";
   $stmt = $dbh->prepare($query);
   $stmt->execute(array($catName));
   // If this category already exists then..
   if ($stmt->rowCount()) {
   $result = $stmt->fetch(PDO::FETCH_ASSOC);
   // Push it in an array to be used outside the loop
   $catIds[] = $result['id'];
   continue;
  }

   $stmt = $dbh->prepare("INSERT INTO categories (name)
   VALUES (?)");
   $stmt->execute(array($catName));
   $catIds[] = $dbh->lastInsertId();
  }
 }
```

What just happened?

We added code to check if the item being inserted already exists in our table. We used the unique guid for this purpose. guid is unique across all feeds (as per the RSS definition). If a feed item already exists in our database, we simply skipped it.

We did something similar for categories. If a category already exists in our categories table then we need not enter it again. Instead we fetched its id, and used this id in the MVA value for the feed item. So categories are shared across feeds.

However, we still have an issue: when the indexer is run the second time, it will overwrite the previously indexed data. So whenever we run the indexer, the index will get overwritten by the latest feed items. However, we don't want to lose old data (feed items).

For this, we will use a technique called index merging.

Index merging

Index merging is more efficient than indexing the data from scratch, that is, all over again. In this technique we define a delta index in the Sphinx configuration file. The delta index always gets the new data to be indexed. However, the main index acts as an archive and holds data that never changes.

In our Feed Search application the **feed-items** index will act as the main index. We will create this index only once, that is, the first time we run the `indexer`. We will add a delta index called **feed-items-delta,** which will be used for successive `indexer` runs. So the delta index will always hold the new feed items, while the main index will hold the archived ones.

After running the `indexer` for delta, we will merge the delta with the main index. This is done using the `indexer` command itself. The next time delta is indexed, we will again get only the new items in it. This way our main index will keep getting appended with new data as and when delta is merged with it.

Let's see the main+delta scheme in action.

Time for action – adding the delta index

1. Modify the configuration file, `/usr/local/sphinx/etc/feeds.conf`, and add the following (highlighted) code:

```
source feeds
{
   type            = xmlpipe2
   xmlpipe_command  = /usr/bin/php /path/to/webroot/feeds/
makeindex.php
   xmlpipe_field      = title
   xmlpipe_field      = description
   xmlpipe_field      = author
   xmlpipe_attr_timestamp = pub_date
   xmlpipe_attr_multi = category_id
}

source feeds-delta : feeds
{
}

index feed-items
{
   source           = feeds
   path             = /usr/local/sphinx/var/data/feed-items
   charset_type     = utf-8
```

```
}

index feed-items-delta : feed-items
{
  source          = feeds-delta
  path            = /usr/local/sphinx/var/data/feed-items-delta
}


indexer
{
  mem_limit       = 64M
}
```

2. Run the `indexer` on feeds-items-delta index (as root):

```
$ /usr/local/sphinx/bin/indexer -c /usr/local/sphinx/etc/feeds.
conf feed-items-delta
```

```
using config file '/usr/local/sphinx/etc/feeds.conf'...
indexing index 'feed-items-delta'...
collected 40 docs, 0.0 MB
collected 166 attr values
sorted 0.0 Mvalues, 100.0% done
sorted 0.0 Mhits, 100.0% done
total 40 docs, 40002 bytes
total 0.025 sec, 1561846 bytes/sec, 1561.76 docs/sec
total 3 reads, 0.000 sec, 12.8 kb/call avg, 0.0 msec/call avg
total 9 writes, 0.000 sec, 10.5 kb/call avg, 0.0 msec/call avg
```

3. Run the command to merge the delta index with the main index:

```
$ /usr/local/sphinx/bin/indexer -c /usr/local/sphinx/etc/feeds.
conf --merge feed-items feed-items-delta
```

```
using config file '/usr/local/sphinx/etc/feeds.conf'...
merged 3.8 Kwords
merged in 0.020 sec
total 6 reads, 0.000 sec, 5.4 kb/call avg, 0.0 msec/call avg
total 6 writes, 0.000 sec, 27.7 kb/call avg, 0.1 msec/call avg
```

What just happened?

We added a second source and index definition in our Sphinx configuration file. This index acts as the delta index. We derived the delta from our main index. The syntax we used for extending the main index was:

```
source feeds-delta : feeds
```

The syntax will define a source `feeds-delta` and all options will be inherited from the source `feeds`. This is somewhat similar to class inheritance in OOP. We can overwrite any option in feeds-delta, extending the index works in a similar fashion.

We didn't overwrite any option in the delta source. However, we overwrote the `source` and `path` options in feed-items-delta index.

Next, we ran the `indexer` to create delta index. This time only new feed items were fetched (in `makeindex.php`) and indexed in the delta. So delta holds only the new items, while old items are held in the main index.

Following this we ran the `indexer` once again, but this time the motive was to merge the delta with the main index:

```
$ /usr/local/sphinx/bin/indexer -c /usr/local/sphinx/etc/feeds.conf
--merge feed-items feed-items-delta
```

We used the `--merge` option of the `indexer`, and provided the names of `feed-items` and `feed-items-delta`, as destination and source indexes respectively.

Once both our main and delta indexes are configured, we will run the `indexer` on delta every time we want to fetch new items, and then merge the delta with the main. We will only perform search on the main index since it will contain all the items.

Search form

We now have the index ready with us. We need a frontend to perform the search on this index. So what are we waiting for? Let's build the search form. We will give the ability to enter a search term, an author name, and select the categories. Author name and category selection will be optional.

On specifying the search term, we will run a full-text search against our index and present the search results returned by Sphinx. If author name or categories have been specified, then we will filter the search results based on the same characteristics.

Time for action – creating the search form

1. Create a script `/path/to/webroot/feeds/search.php` with the following content:

```php
<?php
/**
 * File: /path/to/webroot/feeds/search.php
 */
include('init.php');
```

```
// Get all the categories and their ids
// This will be used to build the categories filter drop down
$query = "SELECT id, name FROM categories ORDER BY name";
foreach ($dbh->query($query) as $row) {
  $viewVars['cat_list'][$row['id']] = $row['name'];
}


// Render the page
render('search');
```

2. Create the view for the search page at /path/to/webroot/feeds/views/
search.thtml:

```
<!-- File: /path/to/webroot/feeds/views/search.thtml -->
<form action="search.php" method="post">
  <fieldset>
    <legend>Search Feeds</legend>
    <div class="input">
      <label>Search for:</label>
      <input type="text" name="q" value="" />
    </div>
    <div class="input">
      <label>Author:</label>
      <input type="text" name="author" value="" />
    </div>
    <div class="input">
      <label>Category:</label>
      <select multiple="true" size="10" name="categories[]">
        <?php foreach ($viewVars['cat_list'] as $id => $name): ?>
        <option value="<?php echo $id; ?>">
          <?php echo $name; ?></option>
        <?php endforeach; ?>
      </select>
    </div>
    <div class="input">
      <label> </label>
      <input type="submit" value="Search" name="search" />
    </div>
  </fieldset>
</form>
```

3. Open `search.php` in a browser.

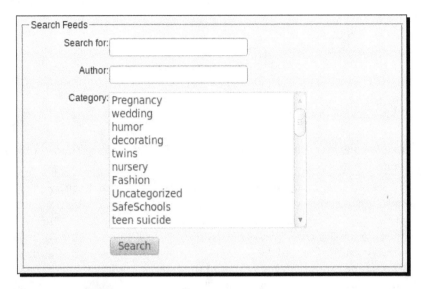

What just happened?

We created a basic form to specify the search phrase, author name, and select multiple categories. We built the categories select box using the category labels we have in our database table.

Search will be performed against different fields as given next:

- ◆ Search for: Required. Full-text search against and description of feed items.
- ◆ Author: Optional. Full-text search against author name in addition to the above.
- ◆ Category: Optional. Filter results by the selected categories in addition to the above.

Perform the search query

The form we created does nothing but render different fields. Let's give it some life by adding the code that performs a search against the Sphinx index and displays the results. We will use a PHP implementation of the Sphinx Client API to perform search queries.

Time for action – adding code to perform a search query

1. Modify the Sphinx configuration file `/var/local/sphinx/etc/feeds.conf` and add section for `searchd`:

```
# Other options (not shown for brevity)
```

```
index feed-items-delta : feed-items
{
  source          = feeds-delta
  path            = /usr/local/sphinx/var/data/feed-items-delta
}

indexer
{
  mem_limit       = 64M
}

searchd
{
  listen          = 9312
  log             = /usr/local/sphinx/var/log/feeds-searchd.log
  query_log       = /usr/local/sphinx/var/log/feeds-query.log
  max_children    = 30
  pid_file        = /usr/local/sphinx/var/log/feeds-searchd.pid
}
```

2. Stop the `searchd` daemon (as root). You need to do this only if `searchd` is already running:

```
$ /usr/local/sphinx/bin/searchd -c /path/to/sphinx.conf --stop
```

3. Start the `searchd` daemon (as root):

```
$ /usr/local/sphinx/bin/searchd -c /usr/local/sphinx/etc/feeds.
conf -i feed-items
```

```
using config file '/usr/local/sphinx/etc/feeds.conf'...
listening on all interfaces, port=9312
```

4. Modify `search.php` and add the following (highlighted) code:

```php
<?php
/**
 * File: /path/to/webroot/feeds/search.php
 */
include('init.php');

// Get the data from post if form is submitted
// else initialize variables to empty strings
$q = !empty($_POST['q']) ? $_POST['q'] : '';
```

```php
$author = !empty($_POST['author']) ? $_POST['author'] : '';
$categories = !empty($_POST['categories']) ? $_POST['categories']
: array();

// Perform the search if we have a search term
if (!empty($q)) {
  do_search($q, $author, $categories);
}

// Get all the categories and their ids
// This will be used to build the categories filter drop down
$query = "SELECT id, name FROM categories ORDER BY name";
foreach ($dbh->query($query) as $row) {
  $viewVars['cat_list'][$row['id']] = $row['name'];
}

// Render the page
render('search');

/**
 * Method to perform the search
 *
 * @param string $q Fulltext search query
 * @param string $author Name of the author
 * @param array $categories Id of the categories for filtering
 */
function do_search($q, $author, $categories)
{
  global $dbh, $viewVars;
  // Include the api class
  require_once('sphinxapi.php');

  $client = new SphinxClient();
  // Set search options
  $client->SetServer('localhost', 9312);
  $client->SetConnectTimeout(1);
  $client->SetArrayResult(true);

  // Set the mode to SPH_MATCH_EXTENDED2
  $client->SetMatchMode(SPH_MATCH_EXTENDED2);
  // Match the search term against title and description
  $query = "@(title,description) ($q)";
```

```
   // Fire the search query against feed-items index (main index)
   $viewVars['results'] = $client->Query($query, 'feed-items');
   $viewVars['items']   = array();

   // Get the item title and link for the matches
   if (!empty($viewVars['results']['matches'])) {
     foreach ($viewVars['results']['matches'] as $match) {
       $itemIds[] = $match['id'];
     }
     $query = "SELECT id, title, link FROM items WHERE id IN (" .
implode(',', $itemIds) . ")";
     $stmt = $dbh->prepare($query);
     $stmt->execute();
     while ($item = $stmt->fetch(PDO::FETCH_ASSOC)) {
       $viewVars['items'][$item['id']] = $item;
     }
   }
 }
}//end do_search()
```

5. Modify the `search.thtml` view and add code to display the results:

```
<!-- File: /path/to/webroot/feeds/views/search.thtml -->
<!-- Code truncated for brevity -->

   <div class="input">
     <label> </label>
     <input type="submit" value="Search" name="search" />
   </div>
  </fieldset>
</form>

<div class="results">
<?php if (isset($viewVars['results']) &&
empty($viewVars['items'])): ?>
  <div class="information">No matching items found!!!</div>
<?php endif; ?>
<?php
if (!empty($viewVars['items'])) {
  print '<div class="information">Total '.$viewVars['results']
['total_found'].' items found</div.';
  print '<ul>';
  foreach ($viewVars['results']['matches'] as $match) {
```

```
         print '<li>
           <a
             href="'.$viewVars['items'][$match['id']]['link'].'">'
           .$viewVars['items'][$match['id']]['title'].'</a></li>';
       }
     print '</ul>';
   }
 ?>
 </div>
```

6. Reload `search.php` in your browser put any term in the **Search for** field, and click on the **Search** button. I searched for 'development' as demonstrated in the following screenshot:

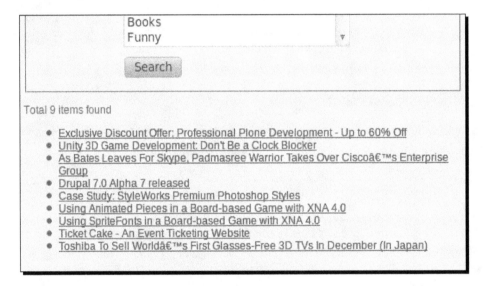

What just happened?

We first added the `searchd` configuration options to the Sphinx configuration file. We specified where to create the log files and what port to listen at. After that, we stopped the `searchd` instance, which was already running. We then started the `searchd` daemon and passed the option `-c` to it so that only the `feed-items` (main) index is served.

After that, we modified the `search.php` script and added code to handle the posted form. We used the `SPH_MATCH_EXTENDED2` match mode so that we can supply a query expression. To search against title and description fields we used `@(title,description) ($q)` expression. This expression reads: 'search all those documents where title and description matches the query'.

Once we get the results from Sphinx, we fetched the respective item's title and link from the feeds table. The document ID returned by Sphinx is the same as the primary key in our `feeds` table.

In the view, we added code to loop through the results and display a list of items hyperlinked to their original pages.

Applying filters

We still haven't added code to perform a search against author name and filter the results by selected categories. So let's do that now.

Time for action – adding code to filter the results

1. Modify the `function do_search()` in `search.php` and add the following highlighted code:

```
function do_search($q, $author, $categories)
{
  global $dbh, $viewVars;
  // Include the api class
  require('sphinxapi.php');

  $client = new SphinxClient();
  // Set search options
  $client->SetServer('localhost', 9312);
  $client->SetConnectTimeout(1);
  $client->SetArrayResult(true);

  // Set the mode to SPH_MATCH_EXTENDED2
  $client->SetMatchMode(SPH_MATCH_EXTENDED2);
  // Match the search term against title and description
  $query = "@(title,description) ($q)";

  // If we have author then match it against author field
  if (!empty($author)) {
    $query .= "@author $author";
  }
  // If categories were selected then filter the results
  if (!empty($categories)) {
    $client->SetFilter('category_id', $categories);
  }
```

```
    // Fire the search query against feed-items index (main index)
    $viewVars['results'] = $client->Query($query, 'feed-items');
    $viewVars['items']   = array();

    // Get the item title and link for the matches
    if (!empty($viewVars['results']['matches'])) {
      foreach ($viewVars['results']['matches'] as $match) {
        $itemIds[] = $match['id'];
      }
      $query = "SELECT id, title, link FROM items
        WHERE id IN (" . implode(',', $itemIds) . ")";
      $stmt = $dbh->prepare($query);
      $stmt->execute();
      while ($item = $stmt->fetch(PDO::FETCH_ASSOC)) {
        $viewVars['items'][$item['id']] = $item;
      }
    }
  }
}//end do_search()
```

What just happened?

We added code to include `author` in the search query if a user has entered the author name in the search form. The final search query looks something like this:

```
@(title,description) ($q) @author $author
```

The search query will match `$q` against the `title` and `description`, and in addition to this the `author` field should also match `$author`.

The second bit of code filters the results by categories. So, only those results that match the full-text query and have the selected categories assigned to them will be finally returned by Sphinx.

We have one final addition to complete our Feed Search application.

Time for action – showing search form prefilled with last submitted data

1. Add the following highlighted code in `search.php`:

```
// Perform the search if we have a search term
if (!empty($q)) {
  do_search($q, $author, $categories);
}
```

```
// Get all the categories and their ids
// This will be used to build the categories filter drop down
$query = "SELECT id, name FROM categories ORDER BY name";
foreach ($dbh->query($query) as $row) {
  $viewVars['cat_list'][$row['id']] = $row['name'];
}

// Assign the search parameters to view variable
$viewVars['q'] = $q;
$viewVars['author'] = $author;
$viewVars['categories'] = $categories;

// Render the page
render('search');
```

2. Modify `search.thtml` and change or add the following highlighted code:

```
      <div class="input">
        <label>Search for:</label>
    <input type="text"
      name="q" value="<?php echo $viewVars['q']; ?>" />
      </div>
      <div class="input">
        <label>Author:</label>
    <input type="text"
      name="author" value="<?php echo $viewVars['author']; ?>" />
      </div>
      <div class="input">
        <label>Category:</label>
        <select multiple="true" size="10" name="categories[]">
          <?php foreach ($viewVars['cat_list'] as $id => $name): ?>
        <?php
          $selected = '';
          if (in_array($id, $viewVars['categories'])) {
            $selected = ' selected';
          }
        ?>
        <option value="<?php echo $id; ?>"<?php echo $selected;
?>><?php echo $name; ?></option>
          <?php endforeach; ?>
        </select>
      </div>
```

3. Reload the search page and try different search queries. Also, try entering author name and selecting one or more categories.

What just happened?

To give the finishing touches to our application we added code to show the form prefilled with the submitted parameters when search results are displayed.

The final search will look like the following screenshot:

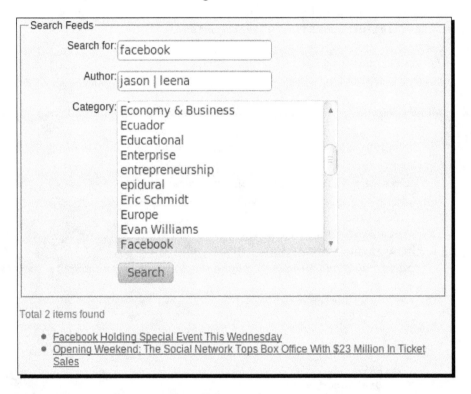

We searched for the term **facebook** against the title and description of feed items. Additionally, we specified that search query should also match **jason** or **leena** against the author field. So, only those items that are authored either by jason or leena will be returned.

Next we filtered the items by **Facebook** category. So the final result will contain only those items which have **Facebook** category assigned to them.

Re-indexing

We now have the index ready with us, and we also have the frontend to perform the search. To fetch new feed items and index them we need to run the following commands at regular intervals:

```
$ /usr/local/sphinx/bin/indexer -c /usr/local/sphinx/etc/feeds.conf feed-
items-delta --rotate
```

```
$ /usr/local/sphinx/bin/indexer -c /usr/local/sphinx/etc/feeds.conf
--merge feed-items feed-items-delta --rotate
```

`--rotate` option is required as the index is already being served by `searchd`. This option creates a second index with the `.new` suffix, parallel to the first, and in the same place. Once the indexing is complete, `indexer` notifies the `searchd` and `searchd` attempts to rename the existing index to include `.old` suffix, and renames `.new` by removing `.new` to replace the existing index.

Have a go hero – trying different search queries

Try adding new feed URLs and re-indexing multiple times. Try different search queries. You can use all the operators mentioned in the Extended Query Syntax section of *Chapter 4, Searching*.

Summary

In this chapter:

- We tried our hand at a practical application that uses a Sphinx backend to perform the core task of searching
- We used PHP for creating an application that fetches different feeds and stores the feed item data in a Sphinx index
- We created a search form that acts as the frontend for searching.
- We learned how to create indexes in the main+delta scheme and how to re-index

In the next chapter we will take up another practical application that will involve some advance features of Sphinx.

6
Property Search

In the previous chapter we saw a very simple application that performed a full-text search on the feed items. In this chapter we will create a more advanced application. So pull up your socks, and get ready to build a complex search application that will search through real estate property listings.

In this chapter we shall:

- ◆ Create a form to add properties
- ◆ Create a form to perform simple full-text search on properties
- ◆ Create an advanced search form
- ◆ Create a form to perform geo-location based searching

So let's get on with it...

The application

This application will search a database of real estate properties. We will create this database and populate it with some data. A property will have the following associated information (fields):

- ◆ Property type
- ◆ Description
- ◆ Price
- ◆ City
- ◆ Address

- ◆ Zip code
- ◆ Number of bedrooms
- ◆ Number of bathrooms
- ◆ Property area
- ◆ Year in which the property was built
- ◆ Geo-coordinates of the property
- ◆ Amenities

We will be creating different search forms; such as a simple, an advanced, and a geo location based search. These forms will have the following characteristics:

- ◆ Simple: A city based filter and full-text search with different weights assigned to each field. We will have a drop-down from which the user can select the city, and a text box to enter search keywords.
- ◆ Advanced: A purely filter based search. We will also use ranged filters in this form. A user will be able to specify the type of property, budget, minimum number of bedrooms, minimum area, and the age of the property as search criteria.
- ◆ Geo location: In this form we will ask for coordinates of the location and search for all nearby properties.

Tools and software used while creating this application

We will be using the following software and tools to build this application:

- ◆ PHP 5.3.2
- ◆ Apache 2.2.14
- ◆ MySQL 5.1.14
- ◆ Sphinx 0.9.9
- ◆ phpMyAdmin (to manage the database)
- ◆ Ubuntu 10.04 LTS
- ◆ Firefox 3.6

We will be building this application on the same lines as we did in the previous chapter. We will use the same HTML/CSS to build our views.

Database structure

Let's get started by creating the database structure. Firstly, we will need a table to hold the property's data; such as type, description, price, number of bedrooms, and so on. We will call this table `properties`.

Each property will be located in a city. It will make sense to normalize the city data so that the same city can be used for multiple properties. To do this, we will create a table `cities` and relate it to the `properties` table.

We will also need to associate amenities (parking, swimming pools, gardens, and so on) to properties. Again we will normalize amenities and keep it in its own table. An amenity can be associated with multiple properties and a property can have multiple amenities. To create such an association we will create a table `amenities_properties`.

Time for action – creating the MySQL database and structure

1. Open phpMyAdmin and create a database `sphinx_properties`. You can use an existing database as well.

2. Import the following SQL to create the database tables:

```
CREATE TABLE IF NOT EXISTS `amenities` (
  `id` int(11) NOT NULL AUTO_INCREMENT,
  `name` varchar(255) NOT NULL,
  PRIMARY KEY (`id`)
) ENGINE=MyISAM  DEFAULT CHARSET=utf8;

CREATE TABLE IF NOT EXISTS `amenities_properties` (
  `amenity_id` int(11) NOT NULL,
  `property_id` int(11) NOT NULL,
  PRIMARY KEY (`amenity_id`,`property_id`)
) ENGINE=MyISAM DEFAULT CHARSET=utf8;

CREATE TABLE IF NOT EXISTS `cities` (
  `id` int(11) NOT NULL AUTO_INCREMENT,
  `name` varchar(255) NOT NULL,
  PRIMARY KEY (`id`)
) ENGINE=MyISAM  DEFAULT CHARSET=utf8;

CREATE TABLE IF NOT EXISTS `properties` (
  `id` int(11) NOT NULL AUTO_INCREMENT,
  `type` enum('1','2') NOT NULL DEFAULT '1',
  `transaction_type` enum('1','2','3') NOT NULL DEFAULT '1',
  `description` text NOT NULL,
```

```
`price` int(11) NOT NULL,
`city_id` int(11) NOT NULL,
`address` text NOT NULL,
`zip_code` varchar(10) NOT NULL,
`bedrooms` int(2) NOT NULL,
`bathrooms` int(2) NOT NULL,
`area` float(10,2) NOT NULL,
`built_year` int(4) NOT NULL,
`latitude` float(5,2) DEFAULT NULL,
`longitude` float(5,2) DEFAULT NULL,
`date_added` datetime NOT NULL,
PRIMARY KEY (`id`)
) ENGINE=MyISAM DEFAULT CHARSET=utf8;
```

What just happened?

We created a new database `sphinx_properties`, which will be used by our application with the following database tables:

◆ `amenities`: This table holds the name of all the amenities related to properties. Search results can be filtered by amenities.

◆ `amenities_properties`: This table holds the data which links a particular amenity to different properties. Each property can have multiple amenities and each amenity can be assigned to multiple properties.

◆ `cities`: This table holds the names of cities. Each property will belong to a city and search results can be filtered by cities.

◆ `properties`: This is the main table that holds the data related to a property. The following fields are added to this table:

  ❑ `type`: Whether the property is Residential (1) or Commercial (2).

  ❑ `transaction_type`: Whether the property is listed for Sale (1), Rent (2), or for a Paying Guest (3).

  ❑ `description`: A description of the property.

  ❑ `price`: The price of the property. (We are keeping this as an integer field.)

  ❑ `city_id`: City where this property is located.

  ❑ `address` and `zip_code`: Address of the property.

  ❑ `bedrooms`, `bathrooms`, and `area`: Characteristics of the property.

  ❑ `built_year`: Year in which this property was built.

  ❑ `latitude` and `longitude`: Geo location of this property.

The following screenshots demonstrate what the database structure will look like:

`amenities` table:

Field	Type	Collation	Attributes	Null	Default	Extra
id	int(11)			No	*None*	auto_increment
name	varchar(255)	utf8_general_ci		No	*None*	

`amenities_properties` table:

Field	Type	Collation	Attributes	Null	Default	Extra
amenity_id	int(11)			No	*None*	
property_id	int(11)			No	*None*	

`cities` table:

Field	Type	Collation	Attributes	Null	Default	Extra
id	int(11)			No	*None*	auto_increment
name	varchar(255)	utf8_general_ci		No	*None*	

`properties` table:

Field	Type	Collation	Attributes	Null	Default	Extra
id	int(11)			No	*None*	auto_increment
type	enum('1','2')	utf8_general_ci		No	1	
transaction_type	enum('1','2','3')	utf8_general_ci		No	1	
description	text	utf8_general_ci		No	*None*	
price	int(11)			No	*None*	
city_id	int(11)			No	*None*	
address	text	utf8_general_ci		No	*None*	
zip_code	varchar(10)	utf8_general_ci		No	*None*	
bedrooms	int(2)			No	*None*	
bathrooms	int(2)			No	*None*	
area	float(10,2)			No	*None*	
built_year	int(4)			No	*None*	
latitude	float(5,2)			Yes	*NULL*	
longitude	float(5,2)			Yes	*NULL*	
date_added	datetime			No	*None*	

Initial data

Now that we have the database structure ready, let's populate the tables with some data.

Frontend for the application

Ideally, you would have a frontend to populate all these tables in a real world application. It is beyond the scope of this book to create a complete frontend for the application.

Time for action – populating the database

Import the following SQL to populate `amenities` and `cities` tables:

```
--
-- Dumping data for table `amenities`
--

INSERT INTO `amenities` (`id`, `name`) VALUES
(1, 'Parking'),
(2, 'Swimming Pool'),
(3, 'Garden'),
(4, 'Elevator'),
(5, 'Club House'),
(6, 'Watchman');


--
-- Dumping data for table `cities`
--

INSERT INTO `cities` (`id`, `name`) VALUES
(1, 'Nagpur'),
(2, 'Mumbai'),
(3, 'New Delhi'),
(4, 'London'),
(5, 'New York'),
(6, 'Hyderabad');
```

What just happened?

We populated the `amenities` and `cities` tables with some data. We did not populate the `properties` table, as we will be creating a simple form to add a property in the next exercise.

Basic setup

We will use the exact same setup as we did in *Chapter 5, Feed Search,* and you can use the same directory structure and common files, such as `init.php`.

Time for action – setting up the application

1. Create a `properties` directory in your webroot, `/path/to/webroot/properties`:

```
$ mkdir /path/to/webroot/properties
```

2. Create the `/path/to/webroot/properties/views` directory:

```
$ mkdir /path/to/webroot/properties/views
```

3. Copy the `sphinxapi.php` file from the Sphinx source directory to the `properties` directory:

```
$ cp /path/to/sphinx-0.9.9/api/sphinxapi.php /path/to/webroot/properties/
```

4. Create the file `/path/to/webroot/properties/init.php` with the following code:

```php
<?php
/**
 * File: /path/to/webroot/properties/init.php
 */
// Database connection credentials
$dsn  ='mysql:dbname=sphinx_properties;host=localhost';
$user = 'root';
$pass = '';

// Instantiate the PDO (PHP 5 specific) class
try {
    $dbh = new PDO($dsn, $user, $pass);
} catch (PDOException $e){
    echo'Connection failed: '.$e->getMessage();
}

// Array to hold variables to be used in views
$viewVars = array();

/**
 * Method to fetch the contents of a view (thtml) file
 * and return the contents.
```

```
     * The html string returned by this method is then
     * placed in the master layout.
     *
     * @param string $view Name of the view file to be fetched.
     *
     * @return string HTML contents specific to the passed view
     */
    function get_view($view)
    {
      global $viewVars;
      // Start the output buffering so that the html output of the
      // view is not sent to the browser immediately.
      ob_start();
      // Include the view file which outputs the HTML
      include("views/$view.thtml");
      // Get the view contents in a variable i.e. whatever the
      // above view outputs, it gets stored in a variable
      $contents = ob_get_contents();
      // Clean the buffer
      ob_end_clean();
      return $contents;
    }//end get_view()


    /**
     * Method to render the page.
     * This method along with get_view()
     * acts as a very simple templating
     * engine and separates the view logic
     * from our php (business) logic.
     *
     * @param string $view Name of the view file to be rendered
     */
    function render($view)
    {
      $contents = get_view($view);
      include('views/layout.thtml');
    }//end render()
```

5. Create the master layout at /path/to/webroot/properties/views/layout.
    thtml:

```
<!-- File: /path/to/webroot/properties/views/layout.thtml -->
<!DOCTYPE html PUBLIC "-//W3C//DTD XHTML 1.0 Transitional//EN"
   "http://www.w3.org/TR/xhtml1/DTD/xhtml1-transitional.dtd">
<html>
```

```
<head>
<title>Property portal</title>
<link rel="stylesheet" type="text/css" href="style.css" />
</head>
<body>
  <div id="header">
    <h1>Property search using Sphinx</h1>
  </div>
  <div id="nav">
    <ul>
      <li><a href="index.php">Home</a></li>
      <li><a href="search.php">Advanced Search</a></li>
      <li><a href="geo_search.php">Geolocation Search</a></li>
      <li><a href="add.php">Add property</a></li>
    </ul>
  </div>
  <div id="content">
    <?php echo $contents; ?>
  </div>
</body>
</html>
```

6. Create /path/to/webroot/properties/style.css:

```
/** File: /path/to/webroot/properties/style.css **/
body {
  font-family: verdana,arial,sans-serif;
  background-color: #F7F5F2;
  font-size: 12px;
  margin: 0;
  overflow: auto;
}
#header {
  text-align: center;
  background-color: #606060;
  color: #ffffff;
  height: 70px;
  padding-top: 5px;
}
#nav ul {
  list-style: none;
  padding: 5px;
  margin: 0px;
}
#nav ul li {
```

```css
    display: inline;
    padding: 5px 10px 5px 10px;
    border-right: 1px solid;
}
#nav {
    background-color: #000000;
    color: #ffffff;
}
#nav a {
    color: #ffffff;
    text-decoration: none;
    font-weight: bold;
}
#content {
    padding: 10px;
}
div.input {
    padding: 5px;
}
label {
    width: 110px;
    text-align: right;
    display: block;
    float: left;
}
.information {
    color: #28630B;
}
```

What just happened?

As in the previous chapter, we created a common PHP file, init.php, which will be used to initialize database connection and contains a few other methods to render the output.

We also created an HTML layout and stylesheet to render the output as a nice looking web page.

 The files created in this exercise were not explained in great detail as they are similar to those created in *Chapter 5, Feed Search*. You should refer to this for further explanation.

At this point your directory structure will look like the following screenshot

```
properties/
|-- init.php
|-- sphinxapi.php
|-- style.css
`-- views
    `-- layout.thtml
```

Adding a property

The next step would be to create a form that will facilitate adding new properties. This form will have fields to specify property details; such as the type of property, city, amenities, and so on.

Time for action – creating the form to add property

_1._ Create a file /path/to/webroot/properties/add.php with the following content:

```php
<?php
/**
 * File: /path/to/webroot/properties/add.php
 */
include('init.php');
// Get the list of cities
$query = "SELECT id, name FROM cities";
foreach ($dbh->query($query) as $row) {
  $viewVars['cities'][$row['id']] = $row['name'];
}

// Get the list of localities
$query = "SELECT id, name FROM localities";
foreach ($dbh->query($query) as $row) {
  $viewVars['localities'][$row['id']] = $row['name'];
}

// Get the list of amenities
$query = "SELECT id, name FROM amenities";
foreach ($dbh->query($query) as $row) {
      $viewVars['amenities'][$row['id']] = $row['name'];
}

// If form is submitted then save the data
// We aren't doing any validation but in a real
```

```php
        // web application you should.
    if (!empty($_POST['description'])) {
        // Query to insert the property
        $query = "INSERT INTO
                properties
                SET
                type = :type,
                transaction_type = :transaction_type,
                description = :description,
                price = :price,
                city_id = :city_id,
                address = :address,
                zip_code = :zip_code,
                bedrooms = :bedrooms,
                bathrooms = :bathrooms,
                area = :area,
                built_year = :built_year,
                latitude = :latitude,
                longitude = :longitude,
                date_added = :date_added";

        $stmt = $dbh->prepare($query);

        $params = array(
                ':type' => strip_tags($_POST['type']),
                ':transaction_type' =>
                    strip_tags($_POST['transaction_type']),
                ':description' => strip_tags($_POST['description']),
                ':price' => (int)$_POST['price'],
                ':city_id' => (int)$_POST['city_id'],
                ':address' => strip_tags($_POST['address']),
                ':zip_code' => strip_tags($_POST['zip_code']),
                ':bedrooms' => (int)$_POST['bedrooms'],
                ':bathrooms' => (int)$_POST['bathrooms'],
                ':area' => (float)$_POST['area'],
                ':built_year' => (int)$_POST['built_year'],
                ':latitude' => (float)$_POST['latitude'],
                ':longitude' => (float)$_POST['longitude'],
                ':date_added' => date('Y-m-d H:i:s'),
                );
        // Execute the statement
        $stmt->execute($params);
        // Get the property id to be used for related amenities
        $property_id = $dbh->lastInsertId();
```

```
   // Insert the amenities
   foreach ($_POST['amenities'] as $amenity) {
     $query = "INSERT INTO
                  amenities_properties
                SET
                  amenity_id = :amenity_id,
                  property_id = :property_id";

     $stmt = $dbh->prepare($query);
     $params = array(
          ':amenity_id' => (int)$amenity,
          ':property_id' => (int)$property_id,
        );
     $stmt->execute($params);
   }
   $viewVars['success'] = true;
}
// Render the view
render('add');
```

2. Create the view for the form at /path/to/webroot/properties/views/add. thtml:

```
<?php if (!empty($viewVars['success'])): ?>
    <div class="information">Property saved successfully</div>
<?php else: ?>
<form action="add.php" method="post">
  <fieldset>
    <legend>Add Property</legend>
    <div class="input">
      <label>Type: </label>
      <input type="radio" name="type" value="1" /> Residential
              
           <input type="radio" name="type" value="2" />Commercial
    </div>
    <div class="input">
      <label>Transaction Type: </label>
      <input type="radio" name="transaction_type" value="1" /> Buy
              
      <input type="radio" name="transaction_type" value="2" />
           Rent
              
      <input type="radio" name="transaction_type" value="3" /> PG
    </div>
```

```html
    <div class="input">
  <label>Description: </label>
  <textarea name="description" rows="5" cols="30"></textarea>
</div>
    <div class="input">
  <label>Price ($): </label>
  <input type="text" name="price" size="5" />
</div>
    <div class="input">
  <label>City: </label>
  <select name="city_id">
      <?php foreach ($viewVars['cities'] as $id => $name): ?>
        <option value="<?php echo $id; ?>">
          <?php echo $name; ?></option>
        <?php endforeach; ?>
        </select>
</div>
    <div class="input">
  <label>Address: </label>
  <textarea name="address"></textarea>
</div>
    <div class="input">
  <label>Zip Code: </label>
  <input type="text" name="zip_code" size="5" />
</div>
    <div class="input">
  <label>Bedrooms: </label>
  <input type="text" name="bedrooms" size="1" />
</div>
    <div class="input">
  <label>Bathrooms: </label>
  <input type="text" name="bathrooms" size="1" />
</div>
    <div class="input">
  <label>Amenities: </label>
  <select name="amenities[]" size="5" multiple>
      <?php
        foreach ($viewVars['amenities'] as $id => $name): ?>
        <option value="<?php echo $id; ?>">
          <?php echo $name; ?>
        </option>
        <?php endforeach; ?>
        </select>
</div>
```

```
        <div class="input">
      <label>Area: </label>
      <input type="text" name="area" size="4" />
    </div>
        <div class="input">
      <label>Built Year: </label>
            <select name="built_year">
            <option value="0">Under Construction</option>
            <?php
                $year = date('Y');
                for ($i = $year; $i >= $year - 200; $i--) {
            ?>
            <option value="<?php echo $i; ?>">
              <?php echo $i; ?></option>
            <?php } ?>
            </select>
    </div>
        <div class="input">
      <label>Latitude: </label>
      <input type="text" name="latitude" size="3" />
    </div>
        <div class="input">
      <label>Longitude: </label>
      <input type="text" name="longitude" size="3" />
    </div>
    <div class="input">
      <label> </label>
      <input type="submit" name="submit" value="Add" />
    </div>
  </fieldset>
</form>
<?php endif; ?>
```

3. Open `add.php` in a browser and add a property with some dummy data, as demonstrated in the following screenshot:

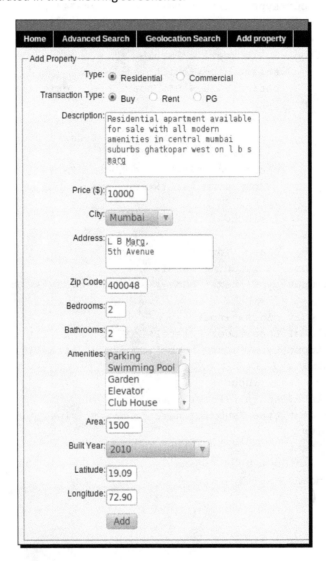

What just happened?

We created a PHP script, `add.php`, in our webroot to add properties. The PHP code is self explanatory.

Next, we created the view, in which we added the HTML form to input data for different fields related to a property.

> **Data validation**
>
> In our code we didn't add any sort of validations. In a real world application you should always add some validations to make sure that form data is not tainted and the field values are what we expected.

Now that we have the form to add a new property, go ahead and add a few dummy properties. For latitude and longitude values you might want to refer to Google maps `http://maps.google.com`.

Indexing the properties

The next step in our application is to index the data using Sphinx's `indexer` tool. We will be creating three separate forms for searching, but the same index will be used by all three search forms.

Time for action – creating the index

1. Create the Sphinx configuration file at `/usr/local/sphinx/etc/properties.conf` with the following content:

```
source properties-source
{
  type           = mysql
  sql_host       = localhost
  sql_user       = root
  sql_pass       =
  sql_db         = sphinx_properties
    sql_query_range = SELECT MIN(id), MAX(id) FROM properties
    sql_range_step  = 1000
    sql_query       = SELECT id, type, \
                    transaction_type, description, \
                    price, city_id, bedrooms, bathrooms, area, \
                    address, zip_code, built_year, \
                    (latitude * PI() / 180) AS latitude, \
                    (longitude * PI() / 180) AS longitude, \
                    UNIX_TIMESTAMP(date_added) AS date_added \
                    FROM properties
                      WHERE id >= $start AND id <= $end
    sql_attr_uint    = type
    sql_attr_uint    = transaction_type
    sql_attr_uint    = price
    sql_attr_uint    = city_id
```

```
        sql_attr_uint       = bedrooms
        sql_attr_uint       = bathrooms
        sql_attr_float       = area
        sql_attr_uint       = built_year
        sql_attr_float       = latitude
        sql_attr_float       = longitude
        sql_attr_timestamp = date_added
    sql_attr_multi       = uint amenity_id from query; \
                SELECT property_id, amenity_id FROM amenities_
properties
}

index properties
{
  source            = properties-source
  path              = /usr/local/sphinx/var/data/properties
  charset_type      = utf-8
}

indexer
{
  mem_limit         = 32M
}

searchd
{
  listen                = localhost:9312
  log                   = /usr/local/sphinx/var/log/searchd.log
  query_log             = /usr/local/sphinx/var/log/query.log
  max_children          = 30
  pid_file              = /usr/local/sphinx/var/log/searchd.pid
}
```

2. Run the `indexer` command to create the index (as root):

/usr/local/sphinx/bin/indexer -c /usr/local/sphinx/etc/properties.conf --all

```
using config file '/usr/local/sphinx/etc/properties.conf'...
indexing index 'properties'...
collected 5 docs, 0.0 MB
collected 10 attr values
sorted 0.0 Mvalues, 100.0% done
sorted 0.0 Mhits, 100.0% done
total 5 docs, 488 bytes
total 0.009 sec, 53964 bytes/sec, 552.91 docs/sec
total 3 reads, 0.000 sec, 0.3 kb/call avg, 0.0 msec/call avg
total 9 writes, 0.000 sec, 0.3 kb/call avg, 0.0 msec/call avg
```

What just happened?

We created the Sphinx configuration file and defined the `source` and `indexer` in it. We are using a MySQL database for this application and defined the `source` options accordingly.

For the first time ever, we used the following options to configure the source. Let's have a look at what each of these options are:

- `sql_query_range`: Is used for ranged document queries. Ranged queries are very useful when indexing lots of data, that is, when the number of records to index goes into millions. This option takes a query that must fetch the minimum and maximum document IDs which will be used as range boundaries. It must return exactly two integer fields in the same order.

  It is because of the ranged query that Sphinx populates two macros, $start and $end, and we need to use: - in `sql_query`, which fetches the actual data. These two macros help in setting up the right conditions to fetch the documents.

- `sql_range_step`: Specifies the steps in document IDs interval. For example, if min and max IDs returned by the `sql_query_range` are 55 and 150 respectively, and if the `sql_range_step` is 40, `indexer` will call `sql_query` three times with the following substitutions for the $start and $end macros:

  - $start = 55, $end = 94
  - $start = 95, $end = 134
  - $start = 135, $end = 150

  So our data gets fetched in three queries instead of one. This is useful if you have lots of records and fetching them all at once may lock MyISAM tables for longer periods, or reduce the performance because of big result sets.

  We fetched all data related to properties in `sql_query`. The geo coordinates, latitude and longitude, are converted from decimal to radians in the query itself. We divide the decimal value by `180/pi`. Sphinx needs them in radians to perform a geo location search (explained more clearly in *Geo distance search* later in this chapter).

- `sql_attr_float` was used to specify the attribute with floating point value. We defined amenity as an MVA because each property can have one or more associated amenities.

The remaining blocks in the configuration file are pretty straightforward and we had used the same settings in our earlier applications.

Lastly, we ran the `indexer` to create the index.

Simple search form

Now let's move on to the crux of our application, the search form. We will start by building a simple search form, wherein the user can select a city and enter a search keyword. This is what most real estate portals provide on their home page, commonly known as a quick search.

Time for action – creating the simple search form

1. Create a script `/path/to/webroot/properties/index.php` with the following content (this will be our home page):

```php
<?php
/**
 * File: /path/to/webroot/properties/index.php
 */
include('init.php');

// Get the list of cities
$query = "SELECT id, name FROM cities";
foreach ($dbh->query($query) as $row) {
  $viewVars['cities'][$row['id']] = $row['name'];
}

// Get the query and city from form (if submitted)
$q = !empty($_POST['q']) ? $_POST['q'] : '';
$city = !empty($_POST['city_id']) ? $_POST['city_id'] : '';

$viewVars['q'] = $q;
$viewVars['city_id'] = $city;
render('index');
```

2. Create the view for the form at `/path/to/webroot/properties/views/index.thtml`:

```html
<form action="index.php" method="post">
  <fieldset>
    <legend>Search</legend>
      <div class="input">
      <label>City: </label>
      <select name="city_id">
          <?php foreach ($viewVars['cities']
            as $id => $name): ?>
          <?php
              $selected = '';
```

```
                    if ($id == $viewVars['city_id']) {
                        $selected = ' selected';
                    }
                ?>
                <option value="<?php echo $id; ?>"
                  <?php echo $selected; ?>>
                  <?php echo $name; ?></option>
                <?php endforeach; ?>
                </select>
        </div>
            <div class="input">
          <label>Search: </label>
          <input type="text" name="q"
            value="<?php echo $viewVars['q']; ?>" />
        </div>
        <div class="input">
          <label> </label>
          <input type="submit" name="submit" value="Search" />
        </div>
        </fieldset>
    </form>
```

What just happened?

We created a form with two fields: a drop-down box to select the city and a textbox to enter the keyword for search.

Search results will be filtered based on the selected city and the search keyword will be matched against the full-text `description`, `address`, and `zip_code` fields.

We have not added the code to perform the actual search query at this point. If you open the `index.php` page in a browser, you will see a search form like the following screenshot:

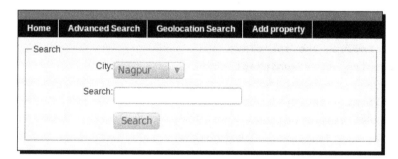

Full-text search

Now let's implement the actual search logic. The keywords entered will be matched against the full-text index and the results will be filtered based on the selected city.

Time for action – adding code to perform full-text search

1. Start the `searchd` daemon (as root):

    ```
    $ /usr/local/sphinx/bin/searchd -c /usr/local/sphinx/etc/
    properties.conf
    ```

    ```
    using config file '../etc/properties.conf'...
    listening on 127.0.0.1:9312
    ```

2. Modify `index.php` and add the following (highlighted) code:

    ```php
    <?php
    /**
     * File: /path/to/webroot/properties/index.php
     */
    include('init.php');

    // Get the list of cities
    $query = "SELECT id, name FROM cities";
    foreach ($dbh->query($query) as $row) {
      $viewVars['cities'][$row['id']] = $row['name'];
    }

    $q = !empty($_POST['q']) ? $_POST['q'] : '';
    $city = !empty($_POST['city_id']) ? $_POST['city_id'] : '';

    // If we have the search term
    if (!empty($q)) {
      // Include the api class
      require_once('sphinxapi.php');

      $client = new SphinxClient();
      // Set search options
      $client->SetServer('localhost', 9312);
      $client->SetConnectTimeout(1);
      $client->SetArrayResult(true);
    ```

```
// Set the mode to SPH_MATCH_ANY
$client->SetMatchMode(SPH_MATCH_ANY);
  // Weights for each field
$weights = array(
            'description' => 1,
            'address' => 10,
            'zip_code' => 50,
          );
$client->SetFieldWeights($weights);

if (!empty($city)) {
  $client->SetFilter('city_id', array($city));
}

$viewVars['results'] = $client->Query($q);
}


$viewVars['q'] = $q;
$viewVars['city_id'] = $city;
render('index');
```

3. Modify the `index.thtml` view and add code to display the results:

```
<!-- File: /path/to/webroot/properties/views/index.thtml -->

    <div class="input">
    <label> </label>
    <input type="submit" name="submit" value="Search" />
  </div>
  </fieldset>
</form>

<div class="results">
<?php if (isset($viewVars['results']) &&
empty($viewVars['results']['matches'])): ?>
  <div class="information">No matching properties found!!!</div>
<?php endif; ?>
<?php
if (!empty($viewVars['results']['matches'])) {
  print '<div class="information">Total '.$viewVars['results']
['total_found'].' properties found</div>';
  print '<ul>';
  foreach ($viewVars['results']['matches'] as $match) {
```

```
         print '<li><a href="view.php?id=' . $match['id']
              . '">Listing #' . $match['id'] .', '
              . $match['attrs']['bedrooms'] . ' Bedrooms '
              . $match['attrs']['area']. 'sq feet, $'
              . $match['attrs']['price']. '</a></li>';
    }
    print '</ul>';
}
?>
</div>
```

4. Reload the `index.php` page in your browser, select any city and search for a term (this depends on the data you provided while adding properties).

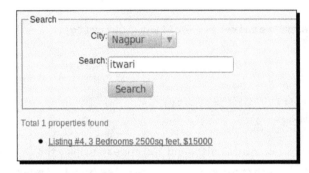

What just happened?

Firstly, we started the `searchd` daemon. If the daemon is already serving another configuration file, then you first need to stop the daemon and then start it for this configuration file. If you try to start two instances of `searchd`, with the same port assigned to the listen option, then you will get an error as shown next:

```
FATAL: failed to lock pid file '/usr/local/sphinx/var/log/searchd.
pid': Resource temporarily unavailable (searchd already running?)
```

We then modified the `index.php` file and added code to handle the search form submission. We used `SPH_MATCH_ANY` matching mode and set weights for each individual fields. We assigned the following weights to the fields:

- `description`—1
- `address`—10
- `zip_code`—50

We assigned the least weight to `description` and the highest weight to the `zip_code` field. This was done so that if a keyword matches the `zip_code` of a document, then that document gets the highest rank, and thus, the `zip_code` field is assigned the maximum weight. Then comes `address` and `description` in that order. We chose the weights so that there is maximum difference between the weights of `description` and `zip_code`. The higher the difference, the higher the weightage.

We used the `SetFieldWeights()` API method, which binds per-field weights by name. The parameter passed to this method is an associative array, mapping string field names to integer weights.

The default value for weight given to each field is 1 and the specified weights must be a positive 32 bit integer.

After adding the search logic, we modified the view to add HTML code in order to display the results.

Have a go hero – try setting different field weights

In `add.php`, try your hand by setting different weights for each field. See how it affects the ranking of results.

Also try other matching modes and see which mode works best for you. Of course, you would first need to add quite a few properties to make the search worthwhile.

Advanced search

Now, let's jump on to a comprehensive search form which will essentially filter search results based on all the attributes; such as city, price, number of bedrooms, area, and so on.

We will build the advanced search form step by step, that is, we will add one filter at a time.

Time for action – creating the Advanced search form

1. Create a script `/path/to/webroot/properties/search.php` with the following content:

```php
<?php
/**
 * File: /path/to/webroot/properties/search.php
 */
include('init.php');

// Get the list of cities
$query = "SELECT id, name FROM cities";
```

```
foreach ($dbh->query($query) as $row) {
  $viewVars['cities'][$row['id']] = $row['name'];
}

// Render the view
render('search');
```

2. Create the view for the search page at `/path/to/webroot/properties/views/search.thtml`:

```html
<form action="advanced_search.php" method="post">
  <fieldset>
    <legend>Advanced search</legend>
        <div class="input">
      <label>City: </label>
      <select name="city_id">
            <?php foreach ($viewVars['cities'] as $id => $name):?>
              <option value="<?php echo $id; ?>">
                <?php echo $name; ?></option>
            <?php endforeach; ?>
      </select>
    </div>
    <div class="input">
      <label>Type: </label>
      <input type="radio" name="type" value="1" checked />
        Residential
               
      <input type="radio" name="type" value="2" /> Commercial
    </div>
    <div class="input">
      <label>Transaction Type: </label>
      <input type="radio"
        name="transaction_type" value="0" checked /> Any
               
      <input type="radio" name="transaction_type" value="1" /> Buy
               
      <input type="radio"
        name="transaction_type" value="2" /> Rent
               
      <input type="radio" name="transaction_type" value="3" /> PG
    </div>
    <div class="input">
      <label> </label>
      <input type="submit" name="submit" value="Search" />
    </div>
  </fieldset>
</form>
```

3. Create a script `/path/to/webroot/properties/advanced_search.php`, with the following content:

```php
<?php
/**
 * File: /path/to/webroot/properties/advanced_search.php
 */
include('init.php');

$city_id = !empty($_POST['city_id']) ? $_POST['city_id'] : '';
$type = !empty($_POST['type']) ? $_POST['type'] : '';
$transaction_type = !empty($_POST['transaction_type']) ? $_POST['transaction_type'] : '';

if (!empty($type)) {
  // Include the api class
  require_once('sphinxapi.php');

  $client = new SphinxClient();
  // Set search options
  $client->SetServer('localhost', 9312);
  $client->SetConnectTimeout(1);
  $client->SetArrayResult(true);

  // Set the mode to SPH_MATCH_FULLSCAN
  // We won't do any full-text search but just filtering
  $client->SetMatchMode(SPH_MATCH_FULLSCAN);

    // Set the type filter
    $client->SetFilter('type', array($type));
    // If we have city filter
    if (!empty($city_id)) {
        $client->SetFilter('city_id', array($city_id));
    }
    // If we have transaction type filter
    if (!empty($transaction_type)) {
        $client->
            SetFilter('transaction_type', array($transaction_type));
    }

    $viewVars['results'] = $client->Query('');
}
render('advanced_search');
```

4. Create the view to display search results at `/path/to/webroot/properties/`
`views/advanced_search.thtml`:

```php
<div class="results">
<?php if (isset($viewVars['results']) &&
empty($viewVars['results']['matches'])): ?>
  <div class="information">No matching properties found!!!</div>
<?php endif; ?>
<?php
if (!empty($viewVars['results']['matches'])) {
  print '<div class="information">
    Total '.$viewVars['results']['total_found'].
    ' properties found</div>';
  print '<ul>';
  foreach ($viewVars['results']['matches'] as $match) {
    print '<li><a href="view.php?id=' . $match['id']
        . '">Listing #' . $match['id'] .', '
        . $match['attrs']['bedrooms'] . ' Bedrooms '
        . $match['attrs']['area']. 'sq feet, $'
        . $match['attrs']['price']. '</a></li>';
  }
  print '</ul>';
}
?>
</div>
```

What just happened?

We started off by creating a form with three search filters: **City**, **Type**, and **Transaction Type**.
The form will be posted on `advanced_search.php`, which will do the actual searching and
display the results.

The form appears as seen in the following screenshot:

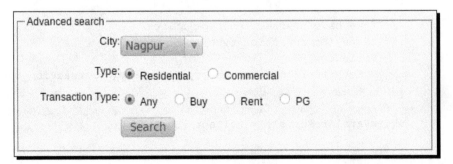

After that, we created `advanced_search.php` and added code to perform the search using the Sphinx client API class. We used `SPH_MATCH_FULLSCAN` matching mode since we only want to perform filtering rather than a full-text search on all documents.

To filter the search results by `city`, `type`, and `transaction_type`, we used the `SetFitler()` method. We didn't pass any term to `Query()` as we are not performing a full-text scan and only doing filtering. We added code so that `SetFilter()` is only called if the respective field has been posted from the form. Lastly, we created the view to display the search results. At this point, try performing searches by selecting different cities, type, and transaction type.

Ranged filters

We want to give a user the ability to perform searches on properties whose price ranges between the specified minimum and maximum values. Similarly, we want to give the user ability to specify a minimum number of bathrooms and bedrooms that the property should have. For searching on ranges of values, we need to use Sphinx's ranged filters. Let's move forward and add ranged filters for different attributes.

Time for action – adding ranged filters

1. Modify `/path/to/webroot/properties/views/search.thtml` as highlighted in the following code:

```html
<!-- File: /path/to/webroot/properties/views/search.thtml -->

        <input type="radio"
          name="transaction_type" value="2" /> Rent
           
        <input type="radio"
          name="transaction_type" value="3" /> PG
  </div>
  <div class="input">
    <label>Budget ($): </label>
    <input type="text" name="min_price" size="5" /> to
    <input type="text" name="max_price" size="5" />
  </div>
  <div class="input">
    <label>Min Bedrooms: </label>
    <input type="text" name="bedrooms" size="1" />
  </div>
  <div class="input">
    <label>Min Bathrooms: </label>
```

```
        <input type="text" name="bathrooms" size="1" />
      </div>
      <div class="input">
        <label>Min Area: </label>
        <input type="text" name="area" size="4" />
      </div>
      <div class="input">
        <label>Max Age: </label>
          <select name="built_year">
          <option value="0">Under Construction</option>
          <option value="<?php echo date('Y'); ?>">
            Current Year</option>
          <?php
              for ($i = 1; $i <= 200; $i++) {
          ?>
          <option value="<?php echo date('Y') - $i; ?>">
            <?php echo $i; ?> Years</option>
          <?php
              }
          ?>
          </select>
      </div>
    <div class="input">
      <label> </label>
      <input type="submit" name="submit" value="Search" />
    </div>
  </fieldset>
</form>
```

2. Modify /path/to/webroot/properties/advanced_search.php and add code to set ranged filters (as highlighted):

```
<?php
/**
 * File: /path/to/webroot/properties/advanced_search.php
 */
include('init.php');

$city_id = !empty($_POST['city_id']) ? $_POST['city_id'] : '';
$type = !empty($_POST['type']) ? $_POST['type'] : '';
$transaction_type = !empty($_POST['transaction_type']) ? $_
POST['transaction_type'] : '';
$min_price = !empty($_POST['min_price']) ? $_POST['min_price'] :
0;
$max_price = !empty($_POST['max_price']) ? $_POST['max_price'] :
0;
$bedrooms = !empty($_POST['bedrooms']) ? $_POST['bedrooms'] : '';
$bathrooms = !empty($_POST['bathrooms']) ? $_POST['bathrooms'] :
```

```php
'';
$area = !empty($_POST['area']) ? $_POST['area'] : '';
$built_year = !empty($_POST['built_year']) ? $_POST['built_year']
: 0;

if (!empty($type)) {
  // Include the api class
  require('sphinxapi.php');

  $client = new SphinxClient();
  // Set search options
  $client->SetServer('localhost', 9312);
  $client->SetConnectTimeout(1);
  $client->SetArrayResult(true);

  // Set the mode to SPH_MATCH_FULLSCAN
  // We won't do any full-text search but just filtering
  $client->SetMatchMode(SPH_MATCH_FULLSCAN);

    // Set the type filter
    $client->SetFilter('type', array($type));
    // If we have city filter
    if (!empty($city_id)) {
        $client->SetFilter('city_id', array($city_id));
    }
    // If we have transaction type filter
    if (!empty($transaction_type)) {
        $client->SetFilter('transaction_type', array($transaction_
type));
    }
    // If we have both min and max price for the budget
    if (!empty($min_price) && !empty($max_price)) {
        $client->SetFilterRange('price', (int)$min_price,
          (int)$max_price);
    }
    // We will assume that max bedrooms can be 10000
    if (!empty($bedrooms)) {
        $client->SetFilterRange('bedrooms', $bedrooms, 10000);
    }

    if (!empty($bathrooms)) {
        $client->SetFilterRange('bathrooms', $bedrooms, 10000);
    }
```

```
    // We will assume that max are can be 99999999.00
    if (!empty($area)) {
        $client->SetFilterFloatRange('area', (float)$area,
            99999999.00);
    }
    // If we have built year then set the range
    if (!empty($built_year)) {
        // Range will be from selected year to current year
        $client->SetFilterRange('built_year', $built_year,
            date('Y'));
    } else {
        // If Under Construction is selected
        //then year attr should be 0
        $client->SetFilter('built_year', array(0));
    }

    $viewVars['results'] = $client->Query('');
}
render('advanced_search');
```

What just happened?

We modified the search form and added search (filter) fields for; budget, minimum number of bedrooms and bathrooms, minimum area of the property, and maximum age of the property.

We then modified the `advanced_search.php` script and added code to collect the form data and apply the respective filters.

Let's try to understand each filter:

- **Budget**: It is made up of minimum price and maximum price. We want to filter the properties that fall under this range. For this we used the `SetFilterRange()` method. That method takes the attribute name as the first argument, and the next two arguments as minimum and maximum values for the range boundary.

- **Bedrooms** and **Bathrooms**: Again we used the `SetFilterRange()` method and passed the value from the form as minimum and kept 10,000 as maximum. Thus we will get only those properties that have at least those many bedrooms or bathrooms. Here we have assumed that maximum number of bedrooms or bathrooms that any property can have is 10,000 (you can adjust this as per your needs).

- **Min Area**: We used the `SetFilterFloatRange()` method in this case. This method works similar to `SetFilterRange()`, with the only difference being that the former should be used for float values and the latter for integer values (attributes).

- **Max Age**: The last filter we added was for the maximum age of the property. We have the `built_year` attribute in the index that holds the year in which the property was built. That attribute holds the value of 0 if the property is under construction. We used conditional logic and applied the correct method to either filter on ranged values or filter for specific value.

The **Advanced search** form (with all the ranged filters) now looks like the following screenshot:

Have a go hero – adding filter for amenities

We added filters for most of the attributes in the previous exercise. The only one remaining was `amenities`, which is a multi-valued attribute in our index.

Go ahead and add a multi select drop-down box in the search form and add related code to filter the search results by amenities. The final search form should appear as seen in the next screenshot:

Geo distance search

The last part of our application is a search form, wherein we can enter the geo coordinates and specify the radius within which the search should be performed. The results should show only those properties which fall under that radius from the specified location (coordinates).

Time for action – creating the search form

1. Create a script `/path/to/webroot/properties/geo_search.php` with the following content:

```php
<?php
/**
 * File: /path/to/webroot/properties/geo_search.php
 */
include('init.php');

// Get the data from form  (if submitted)
$latitude = !empty($_POST['latitude']) ? $_POST['latitude'] : '';
$longitude = !empty($_POST['longitude']) ? $_POST['longitude'] :
'';
$radius = !empty($_POST['radius']) ? $_POST['radius'] : 5;

// Set the variables for view
$viewVars['latitude'] = $latitude;
$viewVars['longitude'] = $longitude;
$viewVars['radius'] = $radius;

render('geo_search');
```

2. Create the view for the geo search page at `/path/to/webroot/properties/views/geo_search.thtml`:

```html
<!-- File: /path/to/webroot/properties/views/geo_search.thtml -->
<form action="geo_search.php" method="post">
  <fieldset>
    <legend>Geo Location Search</legend>
      <div class="input">
    <label>Latitude: </label>
    <input type="text" name="latitude"
      value="<?php echo $viewVars['latitude']; ?>" />
  </div>
      <div class="input">
    <label>Longitude: </label>
    <input type="text" name="longitude"
```

```
              value="<?php echo $viewVars['longitude']; ?>" />
    </div>
        <div class="input">
    <label>Within: </label>
    <select name="radius">
            <?php for ($i = 5; $i <= 30; $i += 5): ?>
            <?php
                $selected = '';
                if ($i == $viewVars['radius']) {
                    $selected = ' selected';
                }
            ?>
            <option value="<?php echo $i; ?>"
              <?php echo $selected; ?>>
              <?php echo "$i Kms"; ?>
            </option>
            <?php endfor; ?>
            </select>
    </div>
    <div class="input">
      <label> </label>
      <input type="submit" name="submit" value="Search" />
    </div>
    </fieldset>
  </form>
```

What just happened?

We created a form with fields able to specify the latitude, longitude, and select a radius (in Kilometers). When opened in a browser, the form appears as follows:

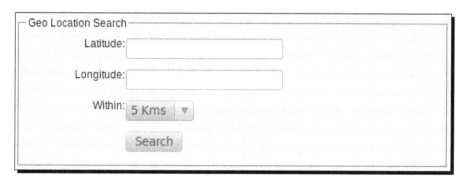

Add geo anchor

Now the last step remaining is adding the code to perform a geo distance based search. So let's do it.

Time for action – adding code to perform geo distance search

1. Modify `/path/to/webroot/properties/geo_search.php` and add the following (highlighted) code:

```php
<?php
/**
 * File: /path/to/webroot/properties/geo_search.php
 */
include('init.php');

// Get the data from form  (if submitted)
$latitude = !empty($_POST['latitude']) ? $_POST['latitude'] : '';
$longitude = !empty($_POST['longitude']) ? $_POST['longitude'] :
'';
$radius = !empty($_POST['radius']) ? $_POST['radius'] : 5;

// If we have coordinates then perform the search
if (!empty($latitude) && !empty($longitude)) {
  // Include the api class
  require_once('sphinxapi.php');

  $client = new SphinxClient();
  // Set search options
  $client->SetServer('localhost', 9312);
  $client->SetConnectTimeout(1);
  $client->SetArrayResult(true);

  // Set the mode to SPH_MATCH_FULLSCAN
  $client->SetMatchMode(SPH_MATCH_FULLSCAN);

    // Convert the latitude and longitude to radians
    $lat  = $latitude * (M_PI / 180);
    $lon = $longitude * (M_PI / 180);

    $client->SetGeoAnchor('latitude', 'longitude', $lat, $lon);
    $rad = $radius * 1000.00; //Convert to meters
    // Set the filter on magic @geodist attribute
```

```php
        $client->SetFilterFloatRange('@geodist', 0.0, $rad);
        // Sort the results by closest distance
        $client->SetSortMode(SPH_SORT_EXTENDED, '@geodist ASC');

        $viewVars['results'] = $client->Query('');
    }


    // Set the variables for view
    $viewVars['latitude'] = $latitude;
    $viewVars['longitude'] = $longitude;
    $viewVars['radius'] = $radius;

    render('geo_search');
```

2. Modify /path/to/webroot/properties/views/geo_search.thtml and add
   code to display the search results (as highlighted):

```html
    <!-- File: /path/to/webroot/properties/views/geo_search.thtml -->

        <div class="input">
          <label> </label>
          <input type="submit" name="submit" value="Search" />
        </div>
        </fieldset>
    </form>
    <div class="results">
    <?php if (isset($viewVars['results']) &&
    empty($viewVars['results']['matches'])): ?>
      <div class="information">No matching properties found!!!</div>
    <?php endif; ?>
    <?php
    if (!empty($viewVars['results']['matches'])) {
      print '<div class="information">
        Total '.$viewVars['results']['total_found'].
        ' properties found</div>';
      print '<ul>';
      foreach ($viewVars['results']['matches'] as $match) {
          $distance = round($match['attrs']['@geodist'] / 1000, 2);
        print '<li><a href="view.php?id=' . $match['id']
            . '">Listing #' . $match['id'] .', '
            . $match['attrs']['bedrooms'] . ' Bedrooms '
            . $match['attrs']['area']. 'sq feet, $'
            . $match['attrs']['price'].
```

```
                ' (' . $distance . ' Kms away)</a></li>';
    }
    print '</ul>';
}
?>
</div>
```

What just happened?

We modified `geo_search.php` and added code to handle the search form submission. We used the `SPH_MATCH_FULLSCAN` matching mode as we only want to filter the documents (without performing full-text search).

To find properties within the selected radius we used the `SetGeoAnchor()` method. This method sets the anchor point for geosphere distance calculations. It takes four arguments in the following order:

1. `$attrlat`: String with the name of the attribute (in index) holding the value for latitude.

2. `$attrlong`: String with the name of the attribute (in index) holding the value for longitude.

3. `$lat`: Float value specifying the anchor point for latitude.

4. `$long`: Float value specifying the anchor point for longitude.

 The latitude and longitude values, both in `SetGeoAnchor()` and the index attribute data, should be in radians.

Whenever an anchor point is set, a magic attribute `@geodist` is attached to the search results. A **magic** attribute means that Sphinx adds this attribute to the result set even though it was not in the index. This attribute holds the geosphere distance between the given anchor point, and the point specified by the latitude and longitude attributes from each match (document). If you print the results array, as returned by Sphinx, you will see the magic attribute.

```
[matches] => Array
    (
        [0] => Array
            (
                [id] => 1
                [weight] => 1
                [attrs] => Array
                    (
                        [type] => 1
                        [transaction_type] => 1
                        [price] => 10000
                        [city_id] => 2
                        [bedrooms] => 2
                        [bathrooms] => 2
                        [area] => 1500
                        [built_year] => 2010
                        [latitude] => 0.33318334817886
                        [longitude] => 1.2723450660706
                        [date_added] => 1287992085
                        [amenity_id] => Array
                            (
                                [0] => 1
                                [1] => 2
                            )

                        [@geodist] => 1114.1510009766
                    )
            )
```

From the previous screenshot you can see that @geodist is attached to the matched document. Once this is done, you can use the magic attribute, just as you would any other attribute, and filter or sort your search results by that attribute.

We filtered the search results using SetFilterFloatRange() on the @geodist attribute. The value of @geodist in matched documents is in meters, hence we converted the value of radius from the form (which is in kilometer) to meters.

We also sorted the search results by the @geodist attribute in ascending order, so that we see the nearest properties at the top. For this we used the SetSortMode() method and used SPH_SORT_EXTENDED mode, which should be used for any magic attribute.

Finally, we modified the view and added code to display the search results. We also added code to show the distance of the matched property from the anchor point.

Have a go hero – adding the delta index using the index merging technique

We used only one index in this property search application. Whenever new properties are added you will have to re-index the whole thing. Re-indexing the already indexed properties can be avoided by implementing the delta index technique that we used in *Chapter 5, Feed Search* (*Index merging* section).

Go ahead and create a delta index and modify the `sql_query` option in the source for delta index so that only those records that are new are fetched. You may want to use the `sql_query_pre` option for marking the records to be indexed, and `sql_query_post_index` for marking the records that were indexed.

Refer to *Chapter 5*, *Feed Search,* for delta indexing and merging.

Summary

In this chapter:

- ◆ We saw some more API methods and explored them. We created an application to search a properties database.

- ◆ We created a simple **Search** form to perform a full-text search on properties and filter them by city. We used different field weights, so that results are sorted with closest matches at the top.

- ◆ We also created an **Advanced search** form where we implemented a lot of filters.

- ◆ We learned how to use ranged filters.

- ◆ We created a search form for **Geo Location Search**. We saw how Sphinx makes it easy to find locations within the specified radius if the index contains geographical coordinates.

In the next chapter we will learn about the Sphinx configuration file and explore some advanced configuration options.

7
Sphinx Configuration

In the earlier chapters we dealt with Sphinx and learnt how it works. We created several indexes and wrote different types of search applications. While doing so we saw the most frequently used Sphinx configuration options.

In this chapter, we will see some more configuration options that will allow you to tailor Sphinx to your needs. There are numerous configuration options available to make Sphinx work exactly the way you want it to. All these are defined in the heart of Sphinx, that is, its configuration file.

Sphinx configuration file

Sphinx has to be configured before we can start using it to create indexes or search. This is done by creating a special configuration file that Sphinx reads while creating an index and searching. The configuration file can be placed anywhere in the file system. The file contains options written in a special format as follows:

```
section_type1 name {
  option11 = value11
  option12 = value12
  option13 = value13
}

section_type2 name {
  option21 = value21
  option22 = value22
  option23 = value23
}
```

Each section has a name and some options, as seen in the previous code snippet. A configuration file can have the following types of sections:

◆ source: Defines the source to fetch the data to be indexed

◆ index: Defines the index properties such as where to save, which charset to use, and so on

◆ indexer: Specifies options to be used by the indexer utility

◆ searchd: Defines the properties of the search daemon, that is, the Sphinx API

Rules for creating the configuration file

What follows are the rules for creating a Sphinx configuration file:

◆ The source and index sections should have a name.

◆ The indexer and searchd sections should not have any name.

◆ source and index can be defined multiple times in a configuration file. However, no two sources or indexes should have the same name.

◆ Source and index can be extended (as done in OOP) using the colon (:) operator. An example would be source delta : main, which means that delta extends main.

◆ There can only be one indexer and one searchd section in the configuration file.

◆ The indexer section is optional. The searchd section is compulsory when using the client API. The source and index sections are compulsory.

◆ Section names can only have letters, numbers, hyphens, and underscores. No spaces.

◆ You can use # to write single line comments.

◆ You can give any name to your configuration file and save it anywhere on your file system. However, it is a good practice to save all configurations in a single directory.

Let's take a look at a few valid and invalid configuration files:

```
# Valid configuration file

source blog {
  type    = mysql
  sql_query = SELECT id, name FROM users
  #...
}

index blog {
  source    = blog
```

```
    path        = /path/to/save/index
}

source childblog : blog {
    sql_query = SELECT id, name FROM users WHERE id > 40
}

index childblog : blog {
    source      = childblog
    path        = /path/to/save/childindex
}

indexer {
    mem_limit   = 32M
}

searchd {
    listen      = localhost:9312
}
```

> Don't worry about the options inside each section. We will take a look at them later in this chapter

The next configuration file is invalid and Sphinx will throw errors when you try to create the index.

```
source blog app {
    #...
}

index blog {
    #...
}

index blog {
    #...
}

searchd blog-daemon {
    #...
}
```

The following errors can be found in the configuration file:

- `source` name contains spaces
- Two indexes have the same name
- `searchd` has a name

If you are developing a web application, save your configuration file outside the webroot. It is recommended to save it in a directory that is not world readable.

Now that we know how to create a Sphinx configuration file and basic rules to create the configuration sections, let's proceed and see what different options can be specified in each section.

Data source configuration

The `source` section is used to define the data source in the configuration file. We learned about data sources in *Chapter 3, Indexing*. Now let's see different configuration options that can be specified in the `source` section of the configuration file.

In this chapter, we will only see those options that are used more often than others and were not already covered in earlier chapters. For complete reference please visit `http://sphinxsearch.com/docs/manual-0.9.9.html#conf-reference`.

SQL related options

We have already seen how to use the basic options; such as `sql_host`, `sql_user`, `sql_pass`, and `sql_db`. There are a few more options that you may need sooner or later.

Connection options

The following options can be used to establish the database connection.

sql_port

If you are using a non-standard port for your database server, then this option is used to specify that port. The default values are; 3306 for mysql source type and 5432 for pgsql type.

sql_sock

For local database server, `sql_host = localhost`, you can specify a UNIX socket name. The default value is `empty`, which means that it will take the value from client library settings.

odbc_dsn

The DSN string used in ODBC connections. This only applies to **odbc** source types and is mandatory if that source type is being used.

Let's create a few sample configuration files with different connection settings.

Here's a sample `source` configuration for MySQL with local server:

```
source src {
  type       = mysql
  sql_host   = localhost
  sql_user   = abbas
  sql_pass   = passwd
  sql_db     = mydb
  sql_sock   = /my/custom/path/mysql.sock
}
```

As shown in the example, at times we may need to explicitly direct Sphinx to where we want it to look for the socket file.

 The MySQL client library will only connect over a UNIX socket if the host is specified as "localhost". If you have specified a remote host or 127.0.0.1, then the connection is established over TCP/IP and `sql_sock` is ignored. A UNIX socket connection is faster than TCP/IP.

Here is a sample with remote host:

```
source src {
  type      = mysql
  sql_host  = 192.168.1.5
  sql_user  = abbas
  sql_pass  = passwd
  sql_db    = mydb
  sql_port  = 3006
}
```

We used a remote host and specified the IP address. In addition, the remote SQL server is running on a non-default port and, as a result, we were needed to specify the port in `sql_port`.

 `sql_port` is not mandatory if using remote host. It should only be used if the host is running on a non-default (3306) port.

Options to fetch data (SQL data source)

In earlier chapters, we have seen the following options to fetch the data when using an SQL data source:

- `sql_query`: Main query to fetch the data to be indexed.
- `sql_query_range`: Used for ranged document fetches. This query must return the maximum and minimum document IDs.
- `sql_range_step`: Specified the range query steps.

Now let's see some other advanced options.

sql_query_pre

The query specified against this option is executed before executing the main `sql_query`. This query is called as **pre-fetch** query.

There can be multiple `sql_query_pre` in a source definition. If more than one pre-fetch query is specified, then they are executed in the order of their appearance in the configuration file.

All results returned by `sql_query_pre` are ignored. `pre` query is generally used to set encoding that the server will use for the rows that it returns, and this encoding must be the same as specified in the `index` section of the Sphinx configuration file.

Another common use of the `pre` query is to mark the records that are going to be indexed, or to update some internal counter. If any errors are returned by the pre-fetch query, they are reported as errors and indexing is terminated.

sql_query_post

This query gets executed immediately after the main `sql_query` completes successfully. This query is called a **post-fetch** query. If any errors are returned by this query, they are reported as warnings and indexing is **not** terminated.

As with `sql_query_pre`, post-fetch query's results are also ignored.

`sql_query_post` should not be used to make any permanent updates to the database. This is because, when this query is executed, indexing is still not complete and it may fail at a later point.

sql_query_post_index

This query is executed after indexing is completed successfully. This query is called a **post-index** query. Any errors produced by this query are reported as warnings and indexing is not terminated. Results returned by this query are ignored.

A macro, $maxid, can be used in this query, and this macro expands to the maximum document ID that was fetched during the indexing.

sql_ranged_throttle

This is the time period (in milliseconds) for which the `indexer` should sleep between ranged fetches. This option comes into play only when using `sql_range_query`. By default no throttling is done.

This option is particularly useful in those cases where the `indexer` may impose too much load on the database server. A carefully selected throttle period will cause the `indexer` to sleep for that period of time after each ranged query step.

Configuration file using advanced options

Let's see an example configuration file using the options that we discussed.

Time for action – creating a configuration with advanced source options

1. Create a database (or use an existing one) with the following structure and data:

```
CREATE TABLE `items` (
`id` INT NOT NULL AUTO_INCREMENT PRIMARY KEY ,
`title` VARCHAR ( 255 ) NOT NULL ,
`content` TEXT NOT NULL ,
`created` DATETIME NOT NULL
) ENGINE = MYISAM ;

CREATE TABLE `last_indexed` (
`id` INT NOT NULL
) ENGINE = MYISAM ;

INSERT INTO `last_indexed` (
```

```
`id`
)
VALUES (
'0'
);
```

2. Add a few rows to the items table so that we get some data to index.

3. Create the Sphinx configuration file /usr/local/sphinx/etc/sphinx-src-
   opt.conf with the following content:

```
source items
{
  type            = mysql
  sql_host        = localhost
  sql_user        = root
  sql_pass        =
  sql_db          = sphinx_conf
  # Set the charset of returned data to utf8
  sql_query_pre       = SET NAMES utf8

  # Turn of the query cache
  sql_query_pre       = SET SESSION query_cache_type = OFF
  sql_query_range     = SELECT MIN(id), MAX(id) FROM items \
                        WHERE id >= (SELECT id FROM last_indexed)
  sql_range_step      = 200

  # Pause for 1000 millisecond (1 sec) between each ranged fetch
  sql_ranged_throttle = 1000

  sql_query  = SELECT id, title, content, created FROM \
               items WHERE id > (SELECT id FROM last_indexed) \
               AND id >= $start AND id <= $end

  # Update the last indexed which will be $maxid
    sql_query_post_index = UPDATE last_indexed SET id = $maxid

  sql_attr_timestamp    = created
}


index items
{
  source          = items
  path            = /usr/local/sphinx/var/data/items
```

```
    charset_type      = utf-8
}
```

4.   Run the `indexer` command:

```
$ /usr/local/sphinx/bin/indexer -c /usr/local/sphinx/etc/sphinx-
src-opt.conf --all
```

```
indexing index 'items'...
collected 201 docs, 0.0 MB
sorted 0.0 Mhits, 100.0% done
total 201 docs, 9010 bytes
total 2.013 sec, 4474 bytes/sec, 99.81 docs/sec
total 2 reads, 0.000 sec, 5.1 kb/call avg, 0.0 msec/call avg
total 7 writes, 0.000 sec, 3.6 kb/call avg, 0.0 msec/call avg
```

What just happened?

We just created two database tables:

◆   `items`—to hold the actual data

◆   `last_indexed`—to hold the id of last indexed item

We then created a configuration file with options, so that main data is fetched in steps of 200, and there is a pause of 1,000 milliseconds (1 second) between each step. This can be easily verified by the output of the `indexer` command, which shows the time taken as **2.013** seconds. In my `items` table I had 201 rows, so the `indexer` paused once before starting for the first time and then after the first 200 records.

We used pre-query to set the encoding that the server will use for the rows it returns. We also turned off query caching in pre-query since `indexer` is not going to run frequently.

Lastly, we used `sql_query_post_index` to increment the id of the last indexed document in the `last_indexed` database table. This is useful for the next indexing, where the main query only fetches those rows which are not already indexed.

MS SQL specific options

The following are a few MS SQL server-specific options

mssql_winauth

This option specifies whether or not to use the account credentials of a currently logged in windows user. This is an optional Boolean option and its default value is 0.

mssql_unicode

This option specifies whether to ask for Unicode or single byte data when querying the MS SQL server. This option must be same as specified in `charset_type` option in the `index` section of the configuration file.

> To index Unicode data, you must set `charset_type` in the `index` section to `utf-8` and `mssql_unicode` to 1 in the `source` section.

This is an optional Boolean option and its default value is 0.

Index configuration

The next mandatory section of the configuration file is the `index` section. This section defines how to index the data and identifies certain properties to look for before indexing the data.

There can be multiple indexes in a single configuration file and an index can extend another index as was done in *Chapter 5, Feed Search*, when we created a main and delta indexing and searching schemes.

There is another powerful searching scheme that should be used if you are indexing billions of records and terabytes of data. This scheme is called distributed searching.

Distributed searching

Distributed searching is useful in searching through a large amount of data, which if kept in one single index would cause high query latency (search time), and will serve a fewer number of queries per second.

In Sphinx, the distribution is done horizontally, that is, a search is performed across different nodes and processing is done in parallel.

To enable distributed searching you need to use `type` option in the index section of the configuration file and set its value to `distributed`.

Set up an index on multiple servers

Let's understand the distributed searching scheme using an example. We will use the same database as we did in our previous exercise. We will use two servers for distribution.

In our example we assume the following:

♦ First (primary) server's IP is `192.168.1.1`

- Second server's IP is `192.168.1.2`
- The database is served from first (`192.168.1.1`) server and both servers use the same database
- The search query will be issued on the first server
- Both servers have Sphinx installed

The set up would appear similar to the next schematic:

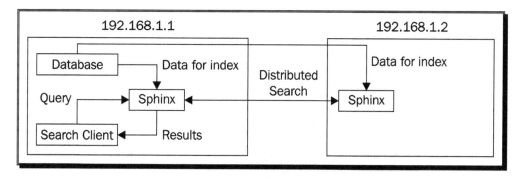

Time for action – creating indexes for distributed searching

1. Create the configuration file on the first server (`192.168.1.1`) at `/usr/local/sphinx/etc/sphinx-distributed.conf` with the following content:

```
source items
{
  type          = mysql
  sql_host      = localhost
  sql_user      = root
  sql_pass      =
  sql_db        = sphinx_conf
  # Query to set MySQL variable @total
  #which holds total num of rows
  sql_query_pre              = SELECT @total := count(id) FROM items
  # Set a variable to hold the sql query
  # We are using CONCAT to use a variable in limit clause
  # which is not possible in direct query execution
  sql_query_pre        = SET @sql = CONCAT('SELECT * FROM items \
                              limit 0,', CEIL(@total/2))
  # Prepare the sql statement
```

```
    sql_query_pre               = PREPARE stmt FROM @sql
    # Execute the prepared statement. This will return rows
    sql_query          = EXECUTE stmt
    # Once documents are fetched, drop the prepared statement
    sql_query_post              = DROP PREPARE stmt

    sql_attr_timestamp     = created
}


index items
{
  source          = items
  path            = /usr/local/sphinx/var/data/items-distributed
  charset_type    = utf-8
}
```

2. Run the `indexer` command to index the data:

    $ /usr/local/sphinx/bin/indexer -c /usr/local/sphinx/etc/sphinx-distributed.conf items

```
indexing index 'items'...
collected 101 docs, 0.0 MB
sorted 0.0 Mhits, 100.0% done
total 101 docs, 4551 bytes
total 0.008 sec, 559159 bytes/sec, 12409.38 docs/sec
total 2 reads, 0.000 sec, 2.7 kb/call avg, 0.0 msec/call avg
total 7 writes, 0.000 sec, 2.0 kb/call avg, 0.0 msec/call avg
```

3. Create the sphinx configuration on the second server (192.168.1.2) at /usr/local/sphinx/etc/sphinx-distributed-2.conf with the following content:

```
source items
{
  type          = mysql
  # we will use remote host (first server)
  sql_host        = 192.168.1.1
  sql_user        = root
  sql_pass        =
  sql_db          = sphinx_conf
  # Query to set MySQL variable @total
  # which holds total num of rows
  sql_query_pre          = SELECT @total := count(id) FROM items
  # Set a variable to hold the sql query
  # We are using CONCAT to use a variable in limit clause
  # which is not possible in direct query execution
```

```
        sql_query_pre      = SET @sql = CONCAT('SELECT * FROM items \
                             limit ', CEIL(@total/2), ',', CEIL(@total/2))
        # Prepare the sql statement
        sql_query_pre      = PREPARE stmt FROM @sql
        # Execute the prepared statement. This will return rows
        sql_query          = EXECUTE stmt
       # Once documents are fetched, drop the prepared statement
       sql_query_post            = DROP PREPARE stmt

       sql_attr_timestamp     = created
    }

    index items-2
    {
      source           = items
      path             = /usr/local/sphinx/var/data/items-2-distributed
      charset_type     = utf-8
    }
```

4. Run the `indexer` on the second server:

$ /usr/local/sphinx/bin/indexer -c /usr/local/sphinx/etc/sphinx-distributed-2.conf items-2

```
indexing index 'items-2'...
collected 100 docs, 0.0 MB
sorted 0.0 Mhits, 100.0% done
total 100 docs, 4459 bytes
total 0.009 sec, 463272 bytes/sec, 10389.61 docs/sec
total 2 reads, 0.000 sec, 2.7 kb/call avg, 0.0 msec/call avg
total 7 writes, 0.000 sec, 1.9 kb/call avg, 0.0 msec/call avg
```

What just happened?

Firstly, we created a configuration on our primary server. This same server has the database and will also host the distributed searching index. However, initially we defined a normal index which uses an SQL source for indexing.

In our source definition we fetched only half the rows from the `items` table. For this we fired a few pre-queries to set the limit and prepare an SQL statement. The following are an explanation of each pre-query:

- First pre-query: Selects the total number of rows from the `items` table and puts the count in a variable `@total`.

- Second pre-query: Sets a string variable holding the query to be executed. The `@total` variable is concatenated after the limit. The query string will look like—`SELECT * FROM items LIMIT 0,101`.

- ◆ Third pre-query: Prepares the statement to be executed based on the query string formed above.

The statement is then executed in the main query, returning the required number of rows. In my case, I had 201 rows in the `items` table. The index created on the primary (`192.168.1.1`) server will contain the first 101 rows (as shown in the output of the `indexer` command).

We then ran the `indexer` thus creating an index with half the amount of data. The remaining half of the rows will be indexed on the second server.

Next, we created a similar configuration file on the second server (`192.168.1.2`). Since both servers will use the same database, we configured the source on the second server to use the database on the primary server . We did this by specifying `192.168.1.1` as the value to the `host` option.

To connect to the MySQL server on `192.168.1.1` from `192.168.1.2`, proper privileges should be assigned on `192.168.1.1`. This can easily be done using a tool such as phpMyAdmin.

We used the same trick again(as in the configuration of the first server) to get the second half of the rows. The final query that got executed for fetching the data was `SELECT * FROM items LIMIT 101, 101`.

Use MySQL stored procedure

Instead of writing so many pre-queries, we could have created a stored procedure to fetch the data in the main query. The stored procedure would set the `@total` variable and prepare the statement, execute it, and return the results.

So, we created indexes on two different servers. The first server has half the data indexed and the second server has the remaining data. Now let's proceed and create a distributed index that will use two indexes to perform a search.

Set up the distributed index on the primary server

The next step is to add a distributed index to the configuration file of the primary server. Let's do it.

Time for action – adding distributed index configuration

1. Modify `/usr/local/sphinx/etc/sphinx-distributed.conf` on the primary server (`192.168.1.1`) and add a new index definition as shown:

```
index master
{
    type        = distributed

    # Local index to be searched
    local      = items

    # Remote agent (index) to be searched
    agent       = 192.168.1.2:9312:items-2
}
```

Modify the configuration files on both `192.168.1.1` and `192.168.1.2` servers, and add the `searchd` section as shown:

```
searchd
{
  log          = /usr/local/sphinx/var/log/searchd-distributed.log
  query_log    = /usr/local/sphinx/var/log/query-distributed.log
  max_children = 30
  pid_file     = /usr/local/sphinx/var/log/searchd-distributed.pid
}
```

2. Start the `searchd` daemon on the primary server (make sure to stop any previous instance):

```
$ /usrl/local/sphinx/bin/searchd -c /usr/local/sphinx/etc/sphinx-
distributed.conf
```

3. Start the `searchd` daemon on the second server (make sure to stop any previous instance):

```
$ /usrl/local/sphinx/bin/searchd -c /usr/local/sphinx/etc/sphinx-
distributed-2.conf
```

What just happened?

We added a second index definition in our configuration file on the primary server. This index will be used for distributed searching. We named this index as `master` and used the `type` option to define it as a distributed index.

The `master` index contains only references to other local and remote indexes. It cannot be directly indexed and is used only for search purposes. You should rather re-index the indexes that `master` references (In our case, the `items` index on the first server and the `items-2` index on the second server).

To reference local indexes, indexes on the same machine or configuration file, `local` option is used. To reference remote indexes, the `agent` option is used. Multiple local and remote indexes can be referenced. For example:

```
local   = items
local   = items-delta

agent   = 192.168.1.2:9312:items-2,items-3
agent   = myhost:9313:items-4
```

We defined two `local` and two `remote` indexes. The syntax for specifying a `remote` index using TCP connection is:

```
hostname:port:index1[,index2[,...]]
```

Syntax for specifying a local UNIX connection is:

```
/var/run/searchd.sock:index4
```

We also added `searchd` configuration section in both the configuration files. Now, if you want to perform a distributed search, you should fire the query against the master index as follows:

```php
<?php
require_once('sphinxapi.php');

$client = new SphinxClient();

$client->SetServer('192.168.1.1', 9312);
$client->SetConnectTimeout(1);
$client->SetArrayResult(true);

$results = $client->Query('search term', 'master');
```

When you send a query to `searchd` using the client API (as shown in the previous code snippet), the following will occur:

- `searchd` connects to the configured remote agents
- It issues the search query
- It searches all local indexes sequentially (at this time, remote agents are searching)
- `searchd` retrieves the remote agents' (index's) search results

◆ It merges results from local and remote indexes and removes any duplicates

◆ Finally, the merged results are sent to the client

◆ When you get the results in your application, there is absolutely no difference between results returned by a normal index and a distributed index

As we just saw, scaling Sphinx horizontally is a breeze and even a beginner can do it.

What follows are a few more options that can be used to configure a distributed index.'

agent_blackhole

This option lets you issue queries to remote agents and then forget them. This is useful for debugging purposes since you can set up a separate `searchd` instance and forward the search queries to this instance from your production instance, without interfering with the production work. The production server's `searchd` will try to connect and query the blackhole agent, but it will not wait for the process or results. This is an optional option and there can be multiple blackholes:

```
agent_blackhole = debugserver:9312:debugindex1,debugindex2
```

agent_connect_timeout

The remote agent's connection timeout in milliseconds. It's an optional option and its default value is 1000 ms (1 second):

```
agent_connect_timeout = 2000
```

This option specifies the time period before `searchd` should give up connecting to a remote agent.

agent_query_timeout

The remote agent's query timeout in milliseconds. It's an optional option and its default value is 3000 ms (3 seconds):

```
agent_query_timeout = 5000
```

This option specifies the time period before `searchd` should give up querying a remote agent.

Distributed searching on single server

The example we saw in the previous section used two different servers. The same example can be built on one server with little modifications to the configuration files. All references to the second server (`192.168.1.2`) should be replaced with the primary server (`192.168.1.1`).

The other important change would be the port on which searchd listens. The configuration file for the secondary server should use a different port for listening than the primary server. The same should be reflected in the agent option of master index.

charset configuration

The next set of options in the index section are charset related options. Let's take a look at them.

charset_type

You can specify the character encoding type using this option. The two character encodings, which are widely a used character set, that can be used with Sphinx are **UTF-8** and **Single Byte Character Set (SBCS)**.charset_type is optional and default value is sbcs. Another known value that it can hold is utf-8.

The specified encoding is used while indexing the data, parsing the query and generating the snippets:

```
charset_type = utf-8
```

charset_table

This is one of the most important options in Sphinx's tokenizing process that extracts keywords from the document text or query. This option controls which characters are acceptable and whether to remove the case or not.

There are more than a hundred thousand characters in Unicode (and 256 in sbcs) and the charset table holds the mapping for each of those characters. Each character is mapped to 0 by default, that is, the character does not occur in keywords and it should be treated as a separator. charset_table is used to map all such characters to either themselves, or to their lower case letter so that they are treated as a part of the keyword. charset_table can also be used to map one character to an entirely different character.

When you specify the charset_type as sbcs then the charset_table being used (internally) is:

```
# 'sbcs' defaults for English and Russian
charset_table = 0..9, A..Z->a..z, _, a..z, \
  U+A8->U+B8, U+B8, U+C0..U+DF->U+E0..U+FF, U+E0..U+FF
```

And when utf-8 charset type is used then the table being used is:

```
# 'utf-8' defaults for English and Russian
charset_table = 0..9, A..Z->a..z, _, a..z, \
  U+410..U+42F->U+430..U+44F, U+430..U+44F
```

Default charset table for sbcs and utf-8 can be overwritten in the index section of the configuration file.

The format for specifying the charset_table is a comma-separated list of mappings (as shown in the previous snippet). You can specify a single character as valid, or map one character to its lowercase character or to another character. There are thousands of characters and specifying each one of them in the table would be a tedious task. Further, it will bloat the configuration file and will be unmanageable. To solve this issue Sphinx lets you use syntax shortcuts that map a whole range of characters at once. The list is as follows:

- a—declares a single character as allowed and maps it to itself.
- A->a—declares A as allowed and maps it to the lowercase a. Lowercase a itself is not declared as allowed.
- A..Z—declares all characters in the range (A to Z) as allowed and maps them to themselves. Use a..z for lowercase range.
- A..Z->a..z—declares all characters in the range A to Z as allowed and maps them to lowercase a to z range. Again, lowercase characters are not declared as allowed by this syntax.
- A..Z/2—declares odd characters in the range as allowed and maps them to the even characters. In addition, it declares even characters as allowed and maps them to themselves. Let's understand this with an example. A..Z/2 is equivalent to the following:

  A->B,B->B,C->D,D->D,E->F,F->F,....,Y->Z,Z->Z

 Unicode characters and 8-bit ASCII characters must be specified in the format U+xxx, where xxx is the hexadecimal codepoint number for the character.

Data related options

On many occasions you may want to limit the type of data to be indexed either by words or length. You may also want to filter the incoming text before indexing. Sphinx provides many options to handle all these things. Let's take a look at some of these options.

stopwords

You may want to skip a few words while indexing, that is, those words should not go in the index. Stopwords are meant for this purpose. A file containing all such words can be stored anywhere on the file system and its path should be specified as the value of the stopwords option.

This option takes a list of file paths (comma separated). The Default value is empty.

You can specify multiple `stopwords` files and all of them will be loaded during indexing. The encoding of the `stopwords` file should match the encoding specified in the `charset_type`. The format of the file should be plain text. You can use the same separators as in the indexed data because data will be tokenized with respect to the `charset_table` settings.

To specify `stopwords` in the configuration file:

```
stopwords = /usr/local/sphinx/var/data/stopwords.txt
stopwords = /home/stop-en.txt
```

And the contents of the `stopwords` file should be (for default charset settings):

```
the into a with
```

Stopwords do affect the keyword positions even though they are not indexed. As an example; if "into" is a stopword and a document contains the phrase "put into hand", and another document contains "put hand"; then when an exact phrase "put hand" is searched for, it will return only the later document, even though "into" in the first document is stopped.

min_word_len

This option specifies the minimum length a word should have to be considered as a candidate for indexing. Default value is 1 (index everything).

For example: If `min_word_len` is 3, then the words "at" and "to" won't be indexed. However; "the", "with", and any other word whose length is three or greater than three will be indexed:

```
min_word_len = 3
```

ignore_chars

This option is used when you want to ignore certain characters. Let's take an example of a hyphen (-) to understand this. If you have a word "test-match" in your data, then this would normally go as two different words, "test" and "match" in the index. However, if you specify "-" in `ignore_chars`, then "test-match" will go as one single word ("testmatch") in the index.

 The syntax for specifying `ignore_chars` is similar to `charset_table` but it only allows you to declare the characters and not to map them. In addition, ignored characters must not be present in the `charset_table`.

Example for hyphen (whose codepoint number is AD):

```
ignore_chars = U+AD
```

html_strip

This option is used to strip out HTML markup from the incoming data before it gets indexed. This is an optional option and its default value is 0, that is, do not strip HTML. The only other value this option can hold is 1, that is, strip HTML.

This option only strips the tags and not the content within the tags. For practical purposes this works in a similar way to the `strip_tags()` PHP function:

```
html_strip = 1
```

html_index_attrs

This option is used to specify the list of HTML attributes whose value should be indexed when stripping HTML.

This is useful for tags, such as `<img>` and `<a>`, where you may want to index the value of the `alt` and `title` attributes:

```
html_index_attrs = img=alt,title; a=title;
```

html_remove_elements

This option is used to specify the list of HTML elements that should be completely removed from the data, that is, both tags and their content are removed.

This option is useful to strip out inline CSS and JavaScript if you are indexing HTML pages:

```
html_remove_elements = style, script
```

Word processing options

We often use a variant of the actual word while searching. For example, we search for "run" and we intend that the results should also contain those documents that match "runs", "running", or "ran". You must have seen this in action on search websites such as Google, Yahoo!, and so on. The same thing can be achieved in Sphinx quite easily using morphology and stemming.

Morphology is concerned with wordforms and it describes how words are pronounced. In morphology, **stemming** is the process of transforming words to their base (root) form, that is, reducing inflected words to their stem.

Morphology

Some pre-processors can be applied to the words being indexed to replace different forms of the same word with the base (normalized) form. Let's see how.

The following exercise assumes that your data (items table) has the word "runs" in one or more records. Further,"run" and "running" are not present in the same record where "runs" is present.

Time for action – using morphology for stemming

1. Create the Sphinx configuration file `/path/to/sphinx-stem.conf` as follows:

```
source items
{
  type            = mysql
  sql_host        = localhost
  sql_user        = root
  sql_pass        =
  sql_db          = sphinx_conf
  sql_query       = SELECT id, title, content, created FROM items
  sql_attr_timestamp = created
}


index items
{
  source          = items
  path            = /usr/local/sphinx/var/data/items-morph
  charset_type    = utf-8
  morphology      = stem_en
}
```

2. Run the `indexer` command:

```
$/usr/local/sphinx/bin/indexer -c /path/to/sphinx-stem.conf items
```

3. Search for the word **run** using the command line `search` utility:

```
$/usr/local/sphinx/bin/search -c /path/to/sphinx-stem.conf run
```

```
index 'items': query 'run ': returned 1 matches of 1 total in 0.000 sec

displaying matches:
1. document=1, weight=1, created=Thu Jan  1 06:03:29 1970

words:
1. 'run': 1 documents, 1 hits
```

4. Search for the word **running**:

```
$/usr/local/sphinx/bin/search -c /path/to/sphinx-stem.conf running
```

```
index 'items': query 'running ': returned 1 matches of 1 total in 0.000 sec

displaying matches:
1. document=1, weight=1, created=Thu Jan  1 06:03:29 1970

words:
1. 'run': 1 documents, 1 hits
```

What just happened?

We created a configuration file to test the `morphology` option with the value `stem_en`. We then indexed the data and ran a few searches. Let's try to understand the results.

Firstly we searched for the word **run**. None of the records in our items table have the word **run**. But even then we got a document in the search results. The reason for this is that `documentID 1` has the word **runs** in one of its fields, and when **runs** is normalized, it becomes "run". As we used the `stem_en` morphology pre-processor, all English words are normalized to their base form. Thus "runs" becomes "run".

Similarly in our second search command, we searched for the word **running**. We again got the same `documentID 1` in the result because **running** is normalized to "run"; and then a `search` is done, thus returning `documentID 1`.

morphology

As we saw in the previous example, Sphinx supports applying morphology pre-processors to the indexed data. This option is optional and the default value is empty, that is, it does not apply any pre-processor.

Sphinx comes with built-in English and Russian stemmers. Other built-in pre-processors are **Soundex** and **Metaphone**. The latter two are used to replace words with phonetic codes. Phonetic codes of different words are equal if they sound phonetically similar. For example, if you use Soundex morphology when your indexed data contains the word "gosh", and someone searches for the word "ghosh", then it will match "gosh". This is because these two words are phonetically similar and have the same phonetic code.

 Multiple stemmers can be specified (comma separated) and they are applied in the order that they are listed. Processing stops if one of the stemmers actually modifies the word.

One more option related to morphology is `min_stemming_len`.

min_stemming_len

This option lets us specify the minimum word length at which the stemming is enabled. The default value is 1 and everything is stemmed.

This option is particularly useful in those cases where stemming does not give you the desired results.

Wordforms

There may be occasions where you want to replace a word with an altogether different word when indexing and searching. For example, when someone searches for "walk", the record with "runs" should match, although the two words are quite different. This cannot be accomplished by stemming (morphology).

Wordforms comes to rescue in such a situation. Wordforms are dictionaries applied after tokenizing the incoming text by `charset_table` rules. These dictionaries let you replace one word with another. An Ideal case of usage is bringing different forms of a word to a single normal form. Wordforms are used both during indexing and searching.

Dictionary file for the wordforms should be in a simple plain text format with each line containing source and destination wordforms. the Same encoding should be used for the wordforms file as specified in the `charset_type`. An example wordform file is shown below.

Here's an example wordform file:

```
walks > runs
walked > walk
play station 3 > ps3
playstation 3 > ps3
```

To specify the wordform file in the index section of the configuration file you should use the `wordforms` option:

```
wordforms = /path/to/wordforms.txt
```

 Wordforms are applied prior to stemming by using morphology pre-processor. If a word is modified by the wordforms then stemmers will not be applied at all.

Search daemon configuration

When searching the index from your application, you will be using Sphinx Client API. This API is accessed using the search daemon, `searchd`, that comes bundled with the Sphinx package. We have seen some basic `searchd` options in earlier chapters. Now let's elaborate them.

listen

As we have previously observed, this option lets you specify the IP and port where searchd will listen on. The syntax for listen is:

```
listen = ( address ":" port | path ) [ ":" protocol ]
```

Let's understand this with a few examples:

```
listen = localhost
listen = 192.168.1.1
listen = 9313
listen = domain:9315
listen = /var/run/sphinx.s
```

- ◆ In the first example only hostname was specified. In this case searchd will listen on your default port, that is 9312.

- ◆ The second example is also similar in that we replaced hostname with IP address.

- ◆ In the third example we specified only the port number. Thus searchd will listen on port 9313 on all available interfaces.

- ◆ In the fourth example, searchd will listen only on one interface (denoted by hostname) and the port 9315.

- ◆ In last example, a UNIX socket path is given to listen on.

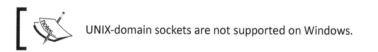 UNIX-domain sockets are not supported on Windows.

You can specify multiple listen directives, and searchd will listen on all specified ports and sockets for the client connections. If no listen option is specified then searchd listens on all interfaces at port 9312.

log

This option specifies the path of the file where our searchd events are logged. The default file is searchd.log:

```
log = /var/log/searchd.log
```

query_log

If specified, this option lets you log the search queries in the specified file, as follows:

```
query_log = /var/log/query.log
```

read_timeout

This option specifies the time period in seconds, before a network read timeout occurs. The default value is 5 seconds, after which searchd will forcibly close the client connections that fail to send a query within five seconds:

```
read_timeout = 3
```

client_timeout

This option specifies the maximum time in seconds, to wait between requests when using persistent connections. Default value is five minutes, or 3,600 seconds:

```
client_timeout = 2400
```

max_children

This option specifies the maximum number of concurrent searches to run in parallel. The default value is 0, which means unlimited connections:

```
max_children = 50
```

This option is particularly useful to control the server load.

pid_file

This is a mandatory option to specify the searchd process ID file name. PID is always re-created and locked when searchd is started, and is unlinked when searchd is shutdown.

Example:

```
pid_file = /usr/local/sphinx/var/searchd.pid
```

max_matches

This option specifies the maximum amount of best matches that the daemon keeps in RAM for each index. The default value is 1,000. Best matches equates to the top matches sorted by specified criteria.

This option is used to limit the RAM usage. Let's understand this with an example. If your query matches 100,000 documents then you would hardly show all those matches. It is a general practice to show only the top few hundred documents. However, all those 100,000 documents will still occupy some space in the RAM, even though you need only a few hundred from them. To tackle this max_matches is used. Max_matches forces searchd to only keep as many matches in RAM as specified.

This limit can be overridden from the API call using the SetLimits() method. However, you can only set the limit to a lower number in the API call than defined in the configuration file, and setting the limit to higher number than max_matches is prohibited:

```
max_matches = 2000
```

seamless_rotate

This option, if enabled, prevents `searchd` from stalling while rotating huge indexes to the precache. The default value is `1`, that is, it is enabled.

Index files that contain the data for attributes, MVA, and keywords, are always precached. If an index is rotated without seamless rotate being enabled, then it tries to use very little RAM and will take some amount of time doing the following:

   ◆   All new queries are temporarily rejected

   ◆   `searchd` waits for all running queries to finish

   ◆   The old index is deallocated and index files are renamed

   ◆   New index files are renamed and required RAM is allocated

   ◆   New index attribute and dictionary data is preloaded to the RAM

   ◆   `searchd` resumes serving queries from new index

If there are a lot of attributes or substantial dictionary data, then the preloading step could take some amount of time (several minutes) in case of large fields.

This can be solved by enabling seamless rotate which does the following:

   ◆   New index RAM storage is allocated

   ◆   New index attribute and dictionary data is asynchronously preloaded to RAM

   ◆   On success, the old index is deallocated and both indexes' files are renamed

   ◆   On failure, the new index is deallocated

   ◆   At any given time, queries are served from either the old or new index copy

Seamless rotate has a few drawbacks in that it uses higher peak memory during the rotation. For example: seamless_rotate = 1

Indexer configuration

These set of options are used when running the `indexer` command to create indexes.

mem_limit

This option specifies the maximum RAM usage limit that the `indexer` will not exceed. The default value is `32M`.

The memory limit can be specified either in bytes, kilo bytes, or mega bytes:

```
mem_limit = 33554432 # 32 MB
```

Here's an example (in kilo bytes):

```
mem_limit = 32768K
```

Here's an example (in mega bytes):

```
mem_limit = 32M
```

max_iops

This option specifies the maximum IO calls per second for I/O throttling. The default value is `0`, which means unlimited:

```
max_iops = 50
```

max_iosize

This option specifies the maximum IO call size in bytes for I/O throttling. The default value is 0, which means unlimited:

```
max_iosize = 1048576
```

max_xmlpipe2_field

This option specifies the maximum length of an `xmlpipe2` field. Default value is 2M:

```
max_xmlpipe2_field = 4M
```

With this we come to the end of configuration options. We left out some options intentionally and those can be referred to in the Sphinx manual (`http://sphinxsearch.com/docs/current.html`).

Summary

In this chapter we learned:

- The basics of creating a Sphinx configuration file
- How to configure the data source to use SQL as well as xmlpipe2 sources
- How to configure Sphinx for distributed searching
- How to use morphology, wordforms, and other data processing options
- How to configure the search daemon and get the most out of it

8
What Next?

So far we have learned pretty much everything about Sphinx and its usage. In this chapter we will explore a few of the newer features that were introduced in recent versions of Sphinx.

We will also see what scenarios Sphinx is useful in, and list a few popular websites that use Sphinx to power their search engines.

SphinxQL

Programmers normally issue search queries using one or more client libraries that relate to the database on which the search is to be performed. Some programmers may also find it easier to write an SQL query than to use the Sphinx Client API library.

SphinxQL is used to issue search queries in the form of SQL queries. These queries can be fired from any client of the database in question, and returns the results in the way that a normal query would. Currently MySQL binary network protocol is supported and this enables Sphinx to be accessed with the regular MySQL API.

SphinxQL in action

Let's take an example of MySQL CLI client program and see how we can use it to query Sphinx. We will use the same database and configuration file that we created in *Chapter 7, Sphinx Configuration* (for distributed searching).

The following exercise uses the **items** database table from *Chapter 7, Sphinx Configuration*.

Time for action – querying Sphinx using MySQL CLI

1. Create the file `/usr/local/sphinx/etc/sphinx-ql.conf` and add the following code:

```
source items
{
  type            = mysql
  sql_host        = localhost
  sql_user        = root
  sql_pass        =
  sql_db          = sphinx_conf
  sql_query       = SELECT id, title, content, \
                        UNIX_TIMESTAMP(created) AS created FROM items
  sql_attr_timestamp  = created
}

index items
{
  source        = items
  path          = /usr/local/sphinx/var/data/items-ql
  charset_type  = utf-8
}

searchd
{
  listen      = localhost:9306:mysql41
  log         = /usr/local/sphinx/var/log/ql-searchd.log
  query_log   = /usr/local/sphinx/var/log/ql-query.log
  pid_file    = /usr/local/sphinx/var/log/ql-searchd.pid
}
```

2. Create the index by running the `indexer` utility:

    $/usr/local/sphinx/bin/indexer -c /usr/local/sphinx/etc/sphinx-ql. conf --all

3. Start the `searchd` daemon:

    $/usr/local/sphinx/bin/searchd -c /usr/local/sphinx/etc/sphinx-ql. conf

4. Connect to the MySQL CLI program:

```
$mysql -u dbuser -pdbpass -h localhost -P 9306
```

5. The previous command will connect to the MySQL server at localhost on port `9306`.

```
Welcome to the MySQL monitor.  Commands end with ; or \g.
Your MySQL connection id is 1
Server version: 0.9.9-release (r2117)

Type 'help;' or '\h' for help. Type '\c' to clear the current input statement.

mysql>
```

6. Issue the following query from MySQL CLI:

```
mysql>SELECT * FROM items WHERE MATCH ('search term');
```

7. The previous query will return the following results:

```
+-------+--------+------------+
| id    | weight | created    |
+-------+--------+------------+
|     2 |   1622 | 1265214529 |
|     3 |   1622 | 1264643742 |
|    10 |   1622 | 1316711694 |
|    11 |   1622 | 1281912160 |
|    25 |   1622 | 1289788601 |
|    43 |   1622 | 1285493374 |
|    76 |   1622 | 1294960894 |
|   100 |   1622 | 1269012635 |
|   121 |   1622 | 1297939962 |
|   158 |   1622 | 1274022492 |
|   180 |   1622 | 1273369297 |
+-------+--------+------------+
11 rows in set (0.00 sec)

mysql>
```

What just happened?

Firstly, we created a new configuration file to index the `items` database table. We put the following value for the `listen` option in `searchd` section of the configuration.

```
listen = localhost:9306:mysql41
```

This line in the configuration enables the MySQL protocol support, and configures Sphinx so that when MySQL client is started at port `9306`, it will use the Sphinx as the server.

mysql41 is the name of the protocol handler to be used when searchd listens on 9306 port. mysql41 is used for MySQL v4.1 up to at least v5.1.

This new access method is supported in addition to the native Sphinx API. You can specify more than one listen options in the searchd section, so that one uses the native API and other the serves the MySQL:

```
listen = localhost:9312
listen = localhost:9306:mysql41
```

We then started the searchd daemon and connected to MySQL CLI. While starting MySQL CLI we used port 9306 , the same port where Sphinx is listening. You would notice that when MySQL gets connected it shows the Sphinx version against the "Server Version", and not the actual MySQL server version. This means that MySQL CLI will now fire queries against Sphinx instead of MySQL server.

After that we fired the following query:

```
mysql>SELECT * FROM items WHERE MATCH ('search term');
```

The query syntax is similar to the MySQL full-text search query syntax. SphinxQL supports the following SQL statements:

- SELECT
- SHOW WARNINGS
- SHOW STATUS
- SHOW META

Let's see the usage of each of these.

SELECT

The SphinxQL syntax adds several Sphinx specific extensions to the regular SQL syntax. Usage of @ symbol for fields in the index and OPTION clause are few Sphinx specific extensions. In addition, there are a few omissions, such as SphinxQL, which does not support JOINs.

Column list clause

Column (field) names, SQL arbitrary expressions, and star (*) are allowed. Some special names, such as @id and @weight , should be used with a leading @ (at-sign). This requirement will be lifted in future versions:

```
SELECT @id AS item_id, category_id, (points + 2)
  AS totalpoints FROM items WHERE MATCH ('search term');
```

Computed expresses must be aliased with a valid unique identifier. For example, `totalpoints` in the previous query. This is unlike SQL where expressions need not have an alias.

FROM clause

The `FROM` clause should contain the list of indexes to be searched. Multiple index names are enumerated by a comma. This is unlike SQL, where comma in `FROM` means `JOIN`:

```
SELECT * FROM items1, items2 WHERE MATCH ('search term');
```

WHERE clause

`WHERE` works for both full-text queries and filters. For filtering, normal comparison operators such as `=`, `!=`, `<`, `>`, `<=`, `>=`, `IN()`, `AND`, `NOT`, and `BETWEEN` are all supported , and these operators map to filters. Full-text search can be performed using the `MATCH()` method, which takes the full-text search query as an argument. The full-text query is interpreted according to the full-text query language rules as explained in *Chapter 4, Searching*.

 The `OR` operator is not supported at the time of writing this book. It will be supported in future versions.

```
SELECT * FROM items WHERE created > 1281912160;
```

This query will get all the documents from the `items` index where the `created` (timestamp) attribute has a value greater than `1281912160`, which is the timestamp for 16th August 2010:

```
SELECT * FROM items
  WHERE MATCH ('search term') AND created > 1281912160;
```

This query will get all the documents where full-text fields match 'search term' and the `created` attribute is greater than `1281912160`:

```
SELECT * FROM items
  WHERE MATCH ('@content (hello | world) @title -bye');
```

This query will search for all documents whose content field matches "hello" or "world", but whose title field does not match "bye".

 There can only be one `MATCH()` in the clause.

GROUP BY clause

Currently only single column grouping is supported. However, the column can be a computed expression.

`AVG()`, `MIN()`, `MAX()`, `SUM()`; functions that are used for aggregating data can be used with either plain attributes or arbitrary expressions as arguments. `GROUP BY` will add an implicit `COUNT(*)` in the form of `@count` column to the result:

```
SELECT *, AVG(points) AS avgpoints FROM items
  WHERE created > 1281912160 GROUP BY category_id;
```

ORDER BY clause

`ORDER BY` works similar to the SQL `ORDER BY` clause, with the difference being that `ASC` and `DESC` are explicitly required, and only column names are allowed and not expressions:

```
SELECT * FROM items WHERE MATCH ('search term')
  ORDER BY created DESC;
```

LIMIT clause

`LIMIT` works exactly similar to the SQL `LIMIT` clause. However, as in the Sphinx API, an implicit `LIMIT 0,20` is always present by default.

> `LIMIT` can not be set to a value greater than `max_matches` config file setting. The maximum number of results Sphinx will fetch will not go over what is set in config file.

```
SELECT * FROM items WHERE MATCH ('@content search_term')
  LIMIT 50;
```

```
SELECT * FROM items WHERE MATCH ('@title search_term')
  LIMIT 50, 100;
```

OPTION clause

This Sphinx-specific extension lets you control a number of per-query options. The options and values are given in the following table:

Option	Values
`ranker`	None, bm25, proximity_bm25, wordcount, proximity, matchany or fieldmask
`max_matches`	integer (per query max matches)
`cutoff`	integer (max found matches threshold)
`max_query_time`	integer (max search time threshold in milliseconds)

Option	Values
`retry_count`	integer (distributed retries count)
`retry_delay`	integer (distributed retry delay in milliseconds)

```
SELECT * FROM items WHERE MATCH ('search term')
  OPTION ranker=bm25, max_matches=5;
```

SHOW WARNINGS

This statement is used to get the warning messages produced by the previous query:

`mysql>SELECT * FROM items WHERE MATCH ('"search term"/3');`

This query will give the following output:

```
+------+--------+------------+
| id   | weight | created    |
+------+--------+------------+
|    2 |   2659 | 1265214529 |
+------+--------+------------+
1 row in set, 1 warning (0.00 sec)

mysql>
```

We searched for "search term" with a quorum threshold value of 3. This gave a result, but with one warning. To retrieve the warning message we can fire the SHOW WARNINGS statement:

`SHOW WARNINGS;`

And it gives the following output:

```
mysql> SHOW WARNINGS;
+---------+------+-------------------------------------------------------------
| Level   | Code | Message
                                   |
+---------+------+-------------------------------------------------------------
| warning | 1000 | quorum threshold too high (words=2, thresh=3); replacing
  quorum operator with AND operator |
+---------+------+-------------------------------------------------------------
1 row in set (0.00 sec)

mysql>
```

This way you can retrieve the warning messages of the latest query.

SHOW STATUS

The following statement shows the performance counters:

```
mysql> SHOW STATUS;
+--------------------+-------+
| Variable_name      | Value |
+--------------------+-------+
| uptime             | 1622  |
| connections        | 1     |
| maxed_out          | 0     |
| command_search     | 0     |
| command_excerpt    | 0     |
| command_update     | 0     |
| command_keywords   | 0     |
| command_persist    | 0     |
| command_status     | 0     |
| agent_connect      | 0     |
| agent_retry        | 0     |
| queries            | 6     |
| dist_queries       | 0     |
| query_wall         | 0.036 |
| query_cpu          | OFF   |
| dist_wall          | 0.000 |
| dist_local         | 0.000 |
| dist_wait          | 0.000 |
| query_reads        | OFF   |
| query_readkb       | OFF   |
| query_readtime     | OFF   |
| avg_query_wall     | 0.006 |
| avg_query_cpu      | OFF   |
| avg_dist_wall      | 0.000 |
| avg_dist_local     | 0.000 |
| avg_dist_wait      | 0.000 |
| avg_query_reads    | OFF   |
| avg_query_readkb   | OFF   |
| avg_query_readtime | OFF   |
+--------------------+-------+
29 rows in set (0.00 sec)
```

SHOW STATUS will show the IO and CPU counters if searchd was started with --iostats and --cpustats switches respectively. The variables returned by SHOW STATUS provide information about the server performance and operation. For example, uptime shows the number of seconds that the server has been running. connections shows the number of attempts that have been made to connect to the server (successful or unsuccessful).

SHOW META

This shows the additional information about the previous query, which includes query time and other statistics:

```
SELECT * FROM items WHERE MATCH ('test');

SHOW META;
```

This query will output the information as shown in the next screenshot:

```
mysql> SELECT * FROM items WHERE MATCH ('test');
+------+--------+------------+
| id   | weight | created    |
+------+--------+------------+
|  101 |   2771 | 1288777387 |
|    2 |   1697 | 1265214529 |
+------+--------+------------+
2 rows in set (0.00 sec)

mysql> SHOW META;
+---------------+-------+
| Variable_name | Value |
+---------------+-------+
| total         | 2     |
| total_found   | 2     |
| time          | 0.000 |
| keyword[0]    | test  |
| docs[0]       | 2     |
| hits[0]       | 3     |
+---------------+-------+
6 rows in set (0.00 sec)
```

So, SHOW META gives the same information that we get in the data returned when we use Sphinx Client API and fire a full-text query.

Use case scenarios

Sphinx can be used in any web application that involves the searching of data. It can be a simple blog, shopping portal, or a very complex hotel or airline booking website. The most common use case of Sphinx is where searching needs to be fast and reliable.

The following is a list of scenarios where Sphinx will perform best:

♦ Applications with a lot (billions of documents) of content
♦ Applications that need to filter their search results based on numerous attributes (which are not full-text)
♦ Applications where search is required on segregated data
♦ Applications where data is coming from a non-conventional source such as a file system, mailboxes, NoSQL databases, and so on
♦ Applications that need distributed searching so that load is balanced

Popular websites using Sphinx

Sphinx is gaining popularity day by day and many high traffic websites are migrating their search engines to Sphinx. A few who have already done this are listed next (Ref: `http://sphinxsearch.com/info/powered/`):

◆ `http://craigslist.org/`: Craigslist is one of the world's most popular and highly visited websites. Thousands of people search the classifieds on craigslist every hour. They moved to using Sphinx in November 2008. Craigslist is known to have the busiest Sphinx server in the world.

◆ `http://www.joomla.org/`: Sphinx is used to improve search through their forum, which comprises more than 700,000 posts.

◆ `http://mininova.org/`: One of the biggest sites to search for torrents. Sphinx on this site servers more than five million searches per day.

◆ `http://boardreader.com/`: The website with the biggest Sphinx installation in terms of data. It is indexing over two billion documents now.

◆ `http://netlog.com/`: This is a huge social networking site with over 35 million users. Search is powered by Sphinx on this site.

◆ `http://www.phpbb.com/`: Sphinx helps index the community area on their site, made up of more than 2.6 million posts.

◆ `http://www.bestcarehome.co.uk` : One of the biggest databases of UK care homes. Uses Sphinx to search through the care homes with complex logic on filtering the searching results based on care needs.

◆ And many more...

Summary

In this chapter:

◆ We learned about SphinxQL, which can be accessed using a regular MySQL client

◆ We saw different statements supported by SphinxQL

◆ We saw different cases when Sphinx can be used

◆ We saw a few popular websites (and some statistics) that use Sphinx

We have covered all the topics that should get you started with using Sphinx in your projects. The beauty of Sphinx is that it is almost language independent. Sphinx client API implementations are available for numerous programming languages.

Index

Symbols

$id macro **41**
$results['matches'] variable **79**
$ which php command **60**
--all argument **47**
& (AND) operator **88**
/indexer command **20**
--prefix configure option **19**
<sphinx:docset> **61**
<sphinx:schema> **61**

A

addresses table **9**
advanced data fetching options
  sql_query_post 186
  sql_query_post_index 187
  sql_query_pre 186
  sql_ranged_throttle 187
advanced search form, property search application
  creating 163-167
advanced source options
  configuration file, creating 187, 189
agent_blackhole option **197**
agent_connect_timeout option **197**
agent_query_timeout option **197**
all-field search operator
  using 93
attributes
  about 37, 50
  adding, to index 50, 52
  adding, to schema 62-67
  characteristics 37
  example 37
  types 37, 38
  uses 37

B

basic search script
  creating 74-78
bin directory **20**
blog
  database tables, creating for 42-45
blog post **38**
BM25 weight **99**
boolean mode queries **86-89**

C

C++ **73**
category_id attribute **55**
charset configuration
  about 198
  options 198, 199
charset configuration, options
  charset_table 198, 199
  charset_type 198
charset_table option **198, 199**
charset_type option **198**
client API implementations, Sphinx **73-78**
client_timeout option **206**
column list clause
  about 212
  FROM 213
  GROUP BY 214
  LIMIT 214
  OPTION 214
  ORDER BY 214
  WHERE 213

configuration file, Sphinx
about 181
creating 45-47
creating, advanced source options used 187,
   189
errors 184
indexer section 182
index section 182
searchd section 182
source section 182
configuration, xmlpipe2 data source 57-61
configure utility
about 12
options 13
Craigslist
about 218
URL 218
cutoff option 214

D

database 36
database connection options
about 184
odbc_dsn 185, 186
sql_port 184
sql_sock 185
database index 35
Database Management System. *See* **DBMS**
database, property search application
populating 144
database structure, property search application
   141
database tables
creating, for blog 42-45
populating 43-45
data fetching options
about 186
sql_query 186
sql_query_range 186
sql_range_step 186
data related options
about 199
html_index_attrs 201
html_remove_elements 201
html_strip 201
ignore_chars 200

min_word_len 200
stopwords 199
data source 38, 39
data source configuration, Sphinx
about 184
SQL related options 184
data source driver 38
DBMS 32
description 23
desktop applications
search 7
display_results() function 82
distributed index
setting up, on primary server 194-196
distributed index configuration
adding 195, 196
distributed index configuration options
about 197
agent_blackhole 197
agent_connect_timeout 197
agent_query_timeout 197
distributed searching
about 190
indexes, creating for 191-193
index, setting up on multiple servers 190-193
performing, on single server 197
duplicate items, feed search application
avoiding, by adding code 122, 123
checking for 122

E

extended query syntax 90-94

F

feed data, feed search application
saving, by adding code 114, 116
feeds
adding, by creating forms 111-114
index, creating 117-122
indexing 117
feed search application
about 105
code, adding to save feed 114, 116
delta index, adding 124-126
duplicate items avoiding, by adding code 122,
   123

duplicate items, checking for 122
feed data, saving 114
feeds application, setting up 108-111
form, creating to add feeds 111
index, creating 117-120
index merging 124
MySQL database and tables, creating 106, 107
re-indexing 137
results filtering, by adding code 133, 134
search form, creating 126-128
search form prefilled with last submitted data, displaying 134-136
search query, performing 128
search query performing, by adding code 128-133
setting up 108-111
software, requisites 106
tools, requisites 106
filter, feed search application
applying 133
results, by applying code 133, 134
search form prefilled with last submitted data, displaying 134-136
filters, property search application
adding, for amenities 171
form, feed search application
creating, to add feeds 111-114
form, property search application
creating, to add property 149,-154
FROM clause 213
full-text search
about 21, 37
advantages 25
applications 25
versus normal search 21-23
full-text search, property search application
performing, by adding code 160-163
full-text search results
filtering 95-98

G

geo distance search, property search application
performing, by adding code 174-178
GROUP BY clause 214
grouping modes, Sphinx
SPH_GROUPBY_ATTR 103

SPH_GROUPBY_DAY 103
SPH_GROUPBY_MONTH 103
SPH_GROUPBY_WEEK 103
SPH_GROUPBY_YEAR 103
grouping search results 103, 104

H

html_index_attrs option 201
html_remove_elements option 201
html_strip option 201

I

ignore_chars option 200
index
about 36
attributes 37, 38
attributes, adding to 50, 52
creating, for distributed searching 191, 192, 193
creating, SQL data source used 41, 42
creating, without attributes 57-60
drawbacks 36
MVA, adding to 52-55
searching 9, 31
setting up, on multiple servers 190-193
index configuration, Sphinx
about 190
charset configuration 198, 199
data related options 199- 201
distributed searching 190
word processing options 201-203
indexer 47
indexer configuration, Sphinx
about 207
max_iops option 208
max_iosize option 208
max_xmlpipe2_field option 208
mem_limit option 207
indexer section, sphinx.conf file 31
indexer utility 25
index, feed search application
creating 117-120
indexing 25-29, 30, 36, 49
index merging, feed search application
about 124
delta index, adding 124-126

index, property search application
  creating 155-157
index, searching
  about 9
  advantage 9
  disadvantage 9
index section, sphinx.conf file 31
installation, Sphinx
  about 11
  issues 14
  system requisites 11
  verifying 19, 20
invalid configuration file 183

L

library 36
LIMIT clause 214
Linux
  Sphinx, installing on 12
listen option 77, 205
live database
  about 8
  search, performing on 8
log option 77, 205
Longest Common Subsequence (LCS) 99
Lucene 32

M

Mac OS X
  Sphinx, installing on 15, 16
main+delta scheme 124
make command 12, 16
master index 196
MATCH() function 24
matching modes, Sphinx
  about 79
  SPH_MATCH_ALL 79
  SPH_MATCH_ANY 79
  SPH_MATCH_BOOLEAN 79
  SPH_MATCH_EXTENDED 79
  SPH_MATCH_EXTENDED2 79
  SPH_MATCH_FULLSCAN 79
  SPH_MATCH_PHRASE 79
max_children option 77, 206
max_iops option 208

max_iosize option 208
max_matches option 206, 214
max_query_time option 214
max_xmlpipe2_field option 208
mem_limit option 207
Metaphone 203
min_stemming_len option 204
min_word_len option 200
morphology
  about 201, 203
  used, for stemming 202, 203
MS SQL server-specific options
  mssql_unicode 190
  mssql_winauth 189
mssql_unicode option 190
mssql_winauth option 189
multiple field search operator
  using 92
Multi-value attributes. *See* **MVA**
MVA
  about 38, 42
  index, adding to 52-55
MyISAM Engine 24
MySQL 39
MySQL CLI
  Sphinx, querying 210-212
MySQL database
  about 8
  addresses table 9
  full-text search 24
  normal search, performing 21-23
  search, performing on 9
  user table 9
MySQL database, feed search application
  creating 106, 107
MySQL database, property search application
  creating 141-143
MySQL structure, property search application
  creating 141-143

N

normal search
  performing, in MySQL 21-23
  versus full-text search 21-23
NOT operator 89

O

odbc_dsn option 185, 186
OPTION clause 214
ORDER BY clause 214
OR operator 88, 213

P

Perl 73
PHP 73
phpMyAdmin 23
phrase search operator
  using 93
pid_file option 77, 206
post-fetch query 186
PostgreSQL 8, 39
post-index query 187
pre-fetch query 186
primary server
  distributed index, setting up on 194-196
property search application
  about 139, 140
  advanced search form, creating 163-167
  database, populating 144
  database structure 141
  delta index adding, index merging technique
      used 178
  filter, adding for amenities 171
  form, creating to add property 149, 151
  form to add property, creating 149
  full-text search performing, by adding code
      160-163
  geo distance search performing, by adding code
      174-178
  index, creating 155-157
  MySQL database, creating 141, 142
  ranged filters, adding 167-170
  search form, creating 172, 173
  setting up 145-148
  simple search form, creating 158, 159
  software, requisites 140
  structure, creating 141-143
  tools, requisites 140
proximity search operator
  using 94

Q

query_log option 77, 205
quorum operator
  using 94

R

ranged filters, property search application
  adding 167-170
ranker option 214
read_timeout option 206
re-indexing, feed search application 137
relevance 24
result set
  filtering 95-98
retry_count option 215
retry_delay option 215
Ruby 73

S

SBCS 198
schema
  attributes, adding to 62-67
  defining, in Sphinx configuration file 67-70
scripting language 23
seamless_rotate option 207
search
  about 7
  performing, on MySQL database 9
search daemon configuration, Sphinx
  about 204
  client_timeout option 206
  listen option 205
  log option 205
  max_children option 206
  max_matches option 206
  pid_file option 206
  query_log option 205
  read_timeout option 206
  seamless_rotate option 207
searchd configuration options
  adding 77
searchd daemon 26, 30, 39, 48, 73, 74, 78
search, desktop applications 7
searchd section, sphinx.conf file 31

search form, feed search application
  creating 126-128
  prefilled with last submitted data, displaying
    134-136
search form, property search application
  creating 172, 173
searching 8, 25-30
search, performing
  ways 8
search query, feed search application
  performing 128
  performing, by adding code 128-133
search utility 41, 48
search, web applications 7
SELECT clause
  about 212
  column list clause 212
  SHOW META statement 216
  SHOW STATUS statement 216
  SHOW WARNINGS statement 215
SELECT query 23
SetFilterFloatRange() method 99
SetFilter() method 98
SetGeoAnchor () method 99
SetGroupBy() API call 103
SetIDRange($min, $max) method 96
SetRankingMode() API method 101
SHOW META statement 216
SHOW STATUS statement 216
SHOW WARNINGS statement 215
simple index
  creating, without attributes 42-45
simple search form, property search application
  creating 158, 159
Single Byte Character Set. *See* SBCS
single server
  distributed searching, performing on 197
Solr 32
sorting modes, Sphinx
  about 102
  SPH_SORT_ATTR_ASC 102
  SPH_SORT_ATTR_DESC 102
  SPH_SORT_EXPR 102
  SPH_SORT_EXTENDED 102
  SPH_SORT_RELEVANCE 102
  SPH_SORT_TIME_SEGMENTS 102

Soundex 203
source section, sphinx.conf file 31
SPH_GROUPBY_ATTR mode 103
SPH_GROUPBY_DAY mode 103
SPH_GROUPBY_MONTH mode 103
SPH_GROUPBY_WEEK mode 103
SPH_GROUPBY_YEAR mode 103
Sphinx
  about 10, 21
  boolean mode queries 86-89
  client API implementations 73-78
  configuration file, creating 31
  data source configuration 184
  extended query syntax 90-94
  features 10
  full-text search 21
  full-text search, advantages 32, 33
  full-text search results, filtering 95-98
  grouping search results 103, 104
  history 10
  index configuration 190
  indexer configuration 207
  indexes 36
  installation, verifying 19, 20
  installing 11, 12
  invalid configuration file 183
  license 11
  matching modes 79-86
  other supported systems 16
  overview 25
  popular websites 218
  querying, MySQL CLI used 210-212
  search daemon configuration 204
  search, using client API 74-78
  search, with different matching modes 80-86
  sorting modes 102
  use case scenarios 217
  used, for indexing 25-30
  used, for searching 25-30
  valid configuration file 182
  weighting search results 99, 100
sphinx:attr element 66
SphinxClient class 78
SphinxClient::Query($query) method 79
SphinxClient::Query() method 86

SphinxClient::SetArrayResult($arrayresult)
    method 79
SphinxClient::SetServer($host, $port) method
    78
sphinx.conf file
  about 31
  indexer section 31
  index section 31
  searchd section 31
  source section 31
Sphinx configuration file
  about 181
  creating 31, 45-47
  indexer section 182
  index section 182
  rules, for creating 182-184
  schema, defining in 67-70
  searchd section 182
  source section 182
Sphinx, installing
  about 11
  issues 14
  on Linux 12
  on Mac OS X 15, 16
  on Windows 14, 15
  system requisites 11
SphinxQL
  SELECT clause 212
  working 209-212
SPH_MATCH_ALL mode 79, 83
SPH_MATCH_ANY mode 79, 83, 101
SPH_MATCH_BOOLEAN mode 79, 101
SPH_MATCH_EXTENDED2 mode 79, 92, 101
SPH_MATCH_EXTENDED mode 79
SPH_MATCH_FULLSCAN mode 79, 83-86
SPH_MATCH_PHRASE mode 79, 83, 85
SPH_SORT_ATTR_ASC mode 102
SPH_SORT_ATTR_DESC mode 102
SPH_SORT_EXPR mode 102
SPH_SORT _EXPR sort mode 37
SPH_SORT_EXTENDED mode 102, 103
SPH_SORT_RELEVANCE mode 102
SPH_SORT_TIME_SEGMENTS mode 102
sql_attr_bigint 41
sql_attr_bool 41
sql_attr_float 41

sql_attr_multi 41, 54
sql_attr_str2ordinal 41
sql_attr_timestamp 41
sql_attr_unit 41
SQL data source
  used, for index creation 41, 42
SQL data sources 39-41
sql_db option 40
sql_host option 40
SQLite 8
sql_* option 31
sql_pass option 40
SQL Phrase Index. *See* Sphinx
sql_port option 40, 184
sql_query option 31, 40, 186
sql_query_post_index option 187
sql_query_post option 186
sql_query_pre option 186
sql_query_range option 186
sql_ranged_throttle option 187
sql_range_step option 186
SQL related options
  about 184
  connection options 184, 186
  data fetching options 186
sql_sock option 185
sql_user option 40
stdout 56
stemming
  about 201
  morphology, using for 202, 203
stopwords option 199
structured documents 36

T

tables, feed search application
  creating 106, 107
tar command 16
test 26, 32
title 23
traditional search 21

U

Use case scenarios 217
users table 9

V

valid configuration file 182
var directory 20

W

web applications
  search 7
webroot 78
weighting 99
weighting functions parts, Sphinx
  about 99
  phrase rank 99
  statistical rank 99
WHERE clause 213
Windows
  Sphinx, installing on 14, 15

wordforms 204
word processing options
  about 201
  morphology 201
  wordforms 204

X

xmlpipe2 data source
  about 39, 56
  configuring 57-61
xmlpipe_command 60
xmlpipe data source 56

Thank you for buying
Sphinx Search Beginner's Guide

About Packt Publishing

Packt, pronounced 'packed', published its first book "*Mastering phpMyAdmin for Effective MySQL Management*" in April 2004 and subsequently continued to specialize in publishing highly focused books on specific technologies and solutions.

Our books and publications share the experiences of your fellow IT professionals in adapting and customizing today's systems, applications, and frameworks. Our solution based books give you the knowledge and power to customize the software and technologies you're using to get the job done. Packt books are more specific and less general than the IT books you have seen in the past. Our unique business model allows us to bring you more focused information, giving you more of what you need to know, and less of what you don't.

Packt is a modern, yet unique publishing company, which focuses on producing quality, cutting-edge books for communities of developers, administrators, and newbies alike. For more information, please visit our website: www.packtpub.com.

About Packt Open Source

In 2010, Packt launched two new brands, Packt Open Source and Packt Enterprise, in order to continue its focus on specialization. This book is part of the Packt Open Source brand, home to books published on software built around Open Source licences, and offering information to anybody from advanced developers to budding web designers. The Open Source brand also runs Packt's Open Source Royalty Scheme, by which Packt gives a royalty to each Open Source project about whose software a book is sold.

Writing for Packt

We welcome all inquiries from people who are interested in authoring. Book proposals should be sent to author@packtpub.com. If your book idea is still at an early stage and you would like to discuss it first before writing a formal book proposal, contact us; one of our commissioning editors will get in touch with you.

We're not just looking for published authors; if you have strong technical skills but no writing experience, our experienced editors can help you develop a writing career, or simply get some additional reward for your expertise.

Joomla! 1.5 SEO

ISBN: 978-1-847198-16-7   Paperback: 324 pages

Improve the search engine friendliness of your web site

1. Improve the rankings of your Joomla! site in the search engine result pages such as Google, Yahoo, and Bing

2. Improve your web site SEO performance by gaining and producing incoming links to your web site

3. Market and measure the success of your blog by applying SEO

Drupal 6 Search Engine Optimization

ISBN: 978-1-847198-22-8   Paperback: 280 pages

Rank high in search engines with professional SEO tips, modules, and best practices for Drupal web sites

1. Concise, actionable steps for increasing traffic to your Drupal site

2. Learn which modules to install and how to configure them for maximum SEO results

3. Create search engine friendly and optimized title tags, paths, sitemaps, headings, navigation, and more

Please check **www.PacktPub.com** for information on our titles

Solr 1.4 Enterprise Search Server

ISBN: 978-1-847195-88-3   Paperback: 336 pages

Enhance your search with faceted navigation, result highlighting, fuzzy queries, ranked scoring, and more

1. Deploy, embed, and integrate Solr with a host of programming languages

2. Implement faceting in e-commerce and other sites to summarize and navigate the results of a text search

3. Enhance your search by highlighting search results, offering spell-corrections, auto-suggest, finding "similar" records, boosting records and fields for scoring, phonetic matching

Expert Python Programming

ISBN: 978-1-847194-94-7   Paperback: 372 pages

Best practices for designing, coding, and distributing your Python software

1. Learn Python development best practices from an expert, with detailed coverage of naming and coding conventions

2. Apply object-oriented principles, design patterns, and advanced syntax tricks

3. Manage your code with distributed version control

4. Profile and optimize your code

Please check **www.PacktPub.com** for information on our titles

www.ingramcontent.com/pod-product-compliance
Lightning Source LLC
Chambersburg PA
CBHW082117070326
40690CB00049B/3601

9 781849 512541